Covert Communication in the Meta Era

In a world increasingly shaped by intelligent and immersive technologies, augmented reality (AR) and artificial intelligence (AI) are redefining how we interact with digital information. This book explores how these powerful tools can be combined with advanced security techniques to create applications that are not only interactive but also secure and discreet.

Bridging theory and practice, the book provides a comprehensive introduction to AR, AI, steganography, and cryptography, guiding readers through their foundations and real-world applications. It examines the evolution of AR technologies and their distinction from virtual and mixed reality, while also presenting key AI concepts with a focus on object detection using modern models such as YOLOv8. The text further explores the principles of steganography and cryptography, highlighting their roles in protecting sensitive information. These concepts are then brought together in the design and development of a dual-purpose augmented reality application. Using Unity and the Vuforia SDK, alongside a custom-trained AI model, the application demonstrates both object recognition for general users and a covert communication system for secure data exchange.

By integrating multiple cutting-edge technologies into a single cohesive framework, this book offers a unique contribution to the field. It is particularly valuable for students, researchers, and professionals seeking practical guidance and innovative approaches to building intelligent, secure AR systems in today's rapidly evolving digital landscape.

Covert Communication in the Meta Era

Blending Steganography with Augmented Reality and Artificial Intelligence

Leila Benarous and Abderrazak Benarous

CRC Press
Taylor & Francis Group
Boca Raton London New York

CRC Press is an imprint of the
Taylor & Francis Group, an **informa** business

First edition published 2027
by CRC Press
2385 NW Executive Center Drive, Suite 320, Boca Raton FL 33431

and by CRC Press
4 Park Square, Milton Park, Abingdon, Oxon, OX14 4RN

CRC Press is an imprint of Taylor & Francis Group, LLC

ISBN: 9781041366546 (hbk)
ISBN: 9781041366553 (pbk)
ISBN: 9781042003860 (ebk)

DOI: 10.1201/9781042003860

Typeset in Times
by KnowledgeWorks Global Ltd.

To our beloved parents,
our cherished brother,
our dear sisters,
our lovely nieces and nephews

Leila & Abderrazak

Contents

List of Abbreviations

AES	Advanced Encryption Standard
AI	Artificial Intelligence
App	Application
AR	Augmented Reality
CIS	Coverless Image Steganography
CNN	Convolutional Neural Network
Colab	Collaboratory
CSP	Cross Stage Partial
DCT	Discrete Cosine Transform
DFT	Discrete Fourier Transform
DWT	Discrete wavelet Transform
GAN	Generative adversarial network
HHO	Harris Hawks optimization
HHO-IWT	Harris Hawks optimization-integer wavelet transform
IoT	Internet of Things
JPEG	Joint Photographic Experts Group
LSB	Least Significant Bit
mAP	mean Average Precision
MR	Mixed Reality
PNG	Portable Network Graphics
PROCAM	Projector and Camera
SIFT	Scale Invariant Feature Transform
SQL	Structured Query Language
starGAN	Star Generative Adversarial Network
VR	Virtual Reality
XR	Extended Reality
YOLO	You Only Look Once

Preface

The rapid development of augmented reality (AR), artificial intelligence (AI), and advanced information security techniques has created exciting opportunities for innovative applications in both everyday technology and research. This book explores the intersection of these fields, focusing on the use of AR and AI for secure communication through steganography and encryption. The primary goal is to demonstrate how seemingly innocuous applications can carry hidden information while maintaining usability and security.

This work is motivated by the growing need for secure and discreet information exchange in the digital era. By combining AR, AI, image steganography, and strong encryption methods, we provide a framework that allows users to hide and reveal secret data in a controlled and reliable manner. The book presents both the theoretical foundations and practical implementations, including a proof-of-concept application that integrates object detection, AR visualization, and secure data handling.

The book is intended for researchers, students, and practitioners interested in AR, AI, cybersecurity, and digital communication. While some familiarity with basic programming, AI concepts, and information security is helpful, the text is designed to be accessible to readers who are new to the combination of these technologies. The chapters are organized to guide the reader from foundational concepts to practical implementation: beginning with an overview of AR and AI technologies, followed by detailed discussions on steganography and cryptography, and concluding with a description of the hybrid AR-based steganography system. Practical examples, illustrations, and analyses are included throughout to support understanding and inspire further exploration.

I hope this book provides both a comprehensive understanding of the potential of AR and AI in secure communications and a source of inspiration for future research in this rapidly evolving field.

Author Biographies

Leila Benarous is an Associate Professor at Amar Telidji University in Laghouat, Algeria, specializing in computer networks, distributed systems, and cybersecurity. Her research focuses on privacy preservation, vehicular networks, and artificial intelligence applications in security. She earned her PhD from Abou Bekr Belkaid University in Tlemcen and obtained her Habilitation to Direct Research in 2025. She has contributed to numerous international publications and holds several patents reflecting her interest in practical and socially relevant innovations. She has also been involved in teaching a wide range of courses in computer science and has participated in academic collaborations with institutions in Algeria and abroad. In addition to her academic work, she is engaged in professional training in networking and cybersecurity. She remains committed to advancing research, education, and innovation in her field.

Abderrazak Benarous is a PhD student in Computer Science, specialty: Networks and Cybersecurity, at the University of Amar Telidji–Laghouat, Algeria. He received his BSc degree in Computer Science (IT Systems and Networks) and his MSc degree in Networks, Distributed Systems, and Applications in 2022 and 2024, respectively, from the University of Amar Telidji–Laghouat, Algeria. His current research focuses on digital forensics and computational intelligence, with a particular emphasis on deepfake detection and analysis. His broader research interests include network security and privacy, distributed and mobile networks, cybersecurity solutions, artificial intelligence for computer vision, steganography and multimedia security, and the integration of emerging technologies such as augmented reality into secure and intelligent systems. He has participated in several national and international scientific events.

General Introduction

We are living in an era of remarkable technological progress, where augmented reality (AR) and artificial intelligence (AI) are emerging as two transformative pillars. AR seamlessly blends digital content with the real world, creating interactive experiences that extend beyond traditional screens, while AI enables systems to solve problems and make decisions by emulating aspects of human intelligence. Together, these technologies open up unprecedented possibilities for both practical applications and research innovation.

At the same time, the need for secure and discreet information exchange has never been greater. Steganography, the art of hiding secret information within ordinary objects, allows data to remain undetectable, while cryptography protects the content itself, ensuring that only those with the correct decryption key can access it. Combining these security techniques with AR and AI provides an opportunity to create systems that are not only interactive but also secure and intelligent.

This book explores precisely this intersection. It presents a comprehensive guide to understanding AR, AI, and modern security techniques, and demonstrates how these concepts can be integrated to develop an augmented reality application with dual functionality. The first function of the application is intended for all users, providing informative descriptions of detected objects within an AR environment. The second function enables covert communication, allowing authorized users to exchange secret information in a secure and concealed manner. Readers will be guided step by step through both the theoretical foundations and the practical development process. The AR environment is built using Unity and the Vuforia SDK, while AI capabilities are implemented through a custom-trained YOLOv8 object detection model. Steganography and cryptography are integrated to ensure secure data embedding and retrieval. Each stage of the application's development – from backend logic and AI training to frontend design and secure data handling – is explained, illustrating how multiple technologies can be combined into a

DOI: 10.1201/9781042003860-1

cohesive system. The structure of the book is designed to gradually build the reader's knowledge and skills:

- **Chapter 1** provides an overview of AR, tracing its history, current applications, and future trends, and clarifies the differences between AR, virtual reality, and mixed reality.
- **Chapter 2** introduces AI, covering its definitions, types, subfields, and object detection techniques, including the YOLOv8 model used in our prototype.
- **Chapter 3** focuses on steganography, exploring its history, modern techniques, applications, and integration with both AI and AR.
- **Chapter 4** presents cryptography, from classic to modern approaches, including hashing and symmetric/asymmetric encryption methods.
- **Chapter 5** discusses the design of a covert communication system for the meta era, highlighting the motivation, methodology, and design considerations.
- **Chapter 6** details the development of a proof-of-concept AR application, describing the backend and frontend implementation, including AR setup, AI integration, and secure data handling through steganography and encryption.

By combining practical guidance with theoretical insights, this book aims to equip readers with the understanding and tools necessary to develop AR applications that are both intelligent and secure. It is intended for students, researchers, and professionals interested in AR, AI, and information security, offering both conceptual knowledge and hands-on experience. Through this work, readers will not only learn how to integrate multiple technologies but also gain a broader understanding of how AR and AI can be leveraged to create innovative and secure applications in today's rapidly evolving digital landscape.

Augmented Reality

1

1.1 INTRODUCTION

Over the last few decades, technology has reshaped the way we live, work and communicate. What began with the personal computer as a tool for calculation and storage evolved into the internet, which connected people and information across the globe. More recently, the rise of artificial intelligence (AI) has added a new layer of capability, enabling systems that learn, adapt and respond to human needs. Alongside these developments, a parallel ambition has taken shape: the desire to move beyond flat screens and keyboards and to interact with digital content in a more natural, spatial way. This pursuit has given rise to immersive technologies that blend the physical and digital worlds.

Virtual reality was among the first to capture widespread attention. By immersing users in entirely computer-generated environments, VR offers a powerful sense of presence but at the cost of disconnecting from the physical world. While this isolation is useful for gaming, simulation, or training, it limits applicability in contexts where awareness of one's surroundings matters. In response, researchers and developers began exploring ways to keep users grounded in reality while still enriching their experience with digital information. This need led to the emergence of augmented reality (AR), a technology that overlays virtual elements onto the real world rather than replacing it. AR does not ask users to leave their environment; instead, it enhances what is already there, adding context, guidance, or hidden layers of information.

This chapter situates AR within that broader technological story. It starts with reviewing its historical development, from early optical experiments to the sophisticated mobile and wearable systems available today. Then, it clarifies how AR differs from related concepts like virtual reality and mixed reality (MR), focusing on the practical implications of each approach. Finally, by the end of this chapter, we look ahead to emerging directions, particularly the growing integration of AR with AI and the Internet of Things (IoT). As these

DOI: 10.1201/9781042003860-2

technologies converge, AR is poised to become more responsive, intuitive and embedded in everyday life. Understanding this evolution helps frame AR not just as a novel interface, but as a promising medium for innovative applications including the secure, context-aware communication systems explored in this research.

1.2 AUGMENTED REALITY HISTORY

AR was first introduced with Pepper's Ghost in 1892, which involved setting up a stage with two distinct rooms: one visible to the audience, and the other hidden either placed on the side or below. A plate of glass is placed at the edge of the stage, angled so that it reflects the view of the second room toward the audience. When the second room is illuminated, its image of the ghost in the room reflects off the glass and appears to them. This staged setup although said to be the initial usage of AR, however, is more like nowadays hologram then like the AR we know today, which is thought of as overlaying images, one is virtual, and the other is a real-world view, done through devices such as goggles or tablets [1].

The English scientists are the ones who attempted the first electronic implementation of AR when they integrated an airborne RADAR navigation system in a WWII de Havilland Mosquito night fighter (a British twin-engine, multirole combat aircraft, introduced during the WWII). In 1971, South Africa and the United States made significant advancements in helmet-mounted gun-sight technology. South Africa was the first air force to operationalize the use of helmet gunsights, while Honeywell Inc. finalized the development of a visor-projected display/tracking system for the US Air Force. This system featured a cathode ray tube (CRT) mounted on the back of the helmet generating the display image, which was then relayed to the front via a coherent fiber optical bundle [1]. Year 1974 marked the first appearance of a visual target acquisition system which consists of a helmet-mounted vision system in US Navy fighter aircraft.

However, AR was not restricted to army use; its application extended beyond that. The entertainment industry quickly recognized its potential and raised people's interest in it; that led to the expansion and the widespread adoption of AR technology. The first use of AR in the entertainment sector was in 1994, when Julie Martin created an AR theater production "Dancing in Cyberspace" [1]. In 1996, Professor Steven Feinberg at Columbia University introduced the first outdoor mobile AR system. In the same year, Sony released a head-mounted display called "Glasstron".

By the late 1990's, AR had become a point of interest to the scientific community; conferences and workshops were held to discuss its progress and evolution. In 1997, Ronald Azuma established its three main elements, which were combining real with virtual, interactivity in real time, and, recording in 3D [2]. **Combining real with virtual** means that AR blends the real-world environment with computer-generated virtual objects, allowing users to interact with both of them. **Interactivity in real time** means that AR systems provide real-time interaction, where virtual objects respond to changes in the real-world environment in real-time. **Recording in 3D** means that those virtual objects appear anchored or aligned correctly within the user's view of the physical world.

In 2004, Mathias Mohring, Christian Lessig and Oliver Bimber managed to put the first AR system on a consumer cell phone [3]. Then, in 2010, Microsoft launched project Baraboo, to develop MR smart glasses. Subsequently, in 2013, car manufacturers began using AR to replace traditional vehicle service manuals. One example of this technology is the Volkswagen MARTA application (Mobile Augmented Reality Assistance), which provides service technicians with detailed information about their vehicles, including diagrams and step-by-step instructions for performing maintenance tasks, while the Audi AR application uses the iPhone camera to provide details about 300 elements in the vehicle, from windscreen wipers to the oil cap [4].

The real milestone that made the buzz, was the release of Metaverse in 2021 by Meta (formerly Facebook). Metaverse expanded social networks to the virtual environment. It is defined as a virtual reality space where users can interact with each other in a computer-generated environment. In 2024, the Apple Vision Pro by Apple, which is an MR mixed reality headset became the talk of the town. It features ultra-high-resolution displays that deliver more pixels than a 4K TV for each eye, allowing users to watch their favorite content on a 100-foot screen [5]; improvements are still in progress to make the AR glasses that are lighter and smarter; some of these glasses are expected to be released in 2026. In Figure 1.1, the evolution of AR from the 1970s to the year 2026 remarking its milestone are depicted. These milestones mark key

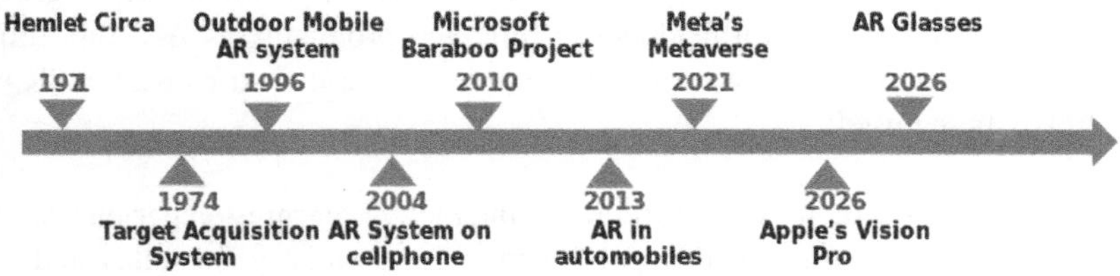

FIGURE 1.1 Historical Overview of AR.

advancements, innovations and developments that have shaped the evolution of AR technology over the decades.

1.3 AR CURRENT APPLICATIONS

AR usage emerged in several fields after it was limited to the military field. Now it is touching various aspects of our lives with its wide range of applications. AR is used to enhance shopping by visualizing products in 3D and virtually allowing clients to try on clothes and shoes to check their fit without the need to wear them. Moreover, it has revolutionized the education system by including 3D visualizations with explanations, animations, simulations and emulations. One of the flourishing AR applications in the education field is medical applications including emulation of the human body and the ability to perform virtual surgeries. These applications are useful to medical students and doctors in their training. Another interesting example is an AR application that showcases chemical reactions in an interesting way that facilitate its understanding and memorization – also, its usage for geography to introduce countries and their cultures, and promote tourism with virtual tours, etc. Additionally, it turns libraries into interactive spaces, where books come to life with 3D illustrations and immersive storytelling.

Apart from its usage in educational and commercial fields, AR is useful in personal utility term as well, like using it to do your daily chores such as organization, cleaning, cooking, etc. AR guides you step by step into cooking delicious recipes, turning you from novice into culinary maestro; it gives you indications on how to fold clothes, sets reminders on when to water your plant or where to place it to grow better, etc. The possibilities are endless, and as the technology continues to develop, so do the applications, with new innovations emerging every day. Thanks to its ability to mix real-world objects with virtual ones, AR is catching the attention of everyone.

In a world where everyone is fascinated by the possibilities of AR, there is no doubt that the demand for innovative applications continues to grow constantly. After all, in a field as dynamic and promising as AR, the limit is our imagination. Below are some examples of the industries where AR is already being used:

- **Education:** It is used to create interactive learning experiences, such as virtual field trips, 3D models, chemistry formulas and immersive simulations. For example: *ITCraft: Pop Up Books.*
- **Healthcare:** It is used for medical training, surgical planning and patient education. For example: Anatomy (AR Anatomy provides a

3D animated AR look at anatomical systems with different pathological conditions).

- **Navigation:** It is used to provide turn-by-turn directions, highlighting points of interest and providing information about the surrounding area. For example: Mercedes-Benz Augmented Reality Navigation [6] and Google Maps [7].
- **Real Estate:** It is used to create virtual tours of properties, allowing customers to explore a property without physically visiting it. For example: realAR.
- **Entertainment:** It is used to create immersive experiences for movies, TV shows and video games. Such as Pokémon Go game [8].

1.4 VIRTUAL REALITY VS MIXED REALITY VS AUGMENTED REALITY

As AR , VR, and MR applications are getting more popular and widely commercialized, people are consuming their applications without necessarily knowing the difference between these three technologies, often mistaking them as one. Indeed, it may be confusing to differentiate between these three terms from a consumer point of view. But from a technical point of view, it is fundamental to do so; therefore, in this section, we explain these technologies and illustrate their use cases with examples to enable you to distinguish between them.

Starting with ***augmented reality***, which indicates that we are extending real-world objects with virtual ones. To formally define it, it is overlaying digitally created content on top of the real world [9]. It enables the user to interact with both the physical world and digital elements. Some AR examples in real life are:

- **Pokémon-go:** It is an AR mobile game, developed and published by Niantic in collaboration with Nintendo and The Pokémon Company for iOS and Android devices. It was a revolutionary game that made the headlines during its release time with 232 million curious players recorded that year. The game idea is to collect Pokémon hidden in real locations; players use their phone's camera to catch and locate them [10].
- **IKEA Place app:** It is an AR application that lets people confidently experience home appliances and interior design decoration in any space before buying the products [11].

- **Google maps:** It includes a reality mode in which arrows are added to guide you to your destination. After selecting this mode, you only have to direct your phone to one of the key landmarks surrounding you, such as a marketplace, a museum, or a gym; then the application would recognize your location and start drawing arrows on the road that you can see virtually from your app indicating where you should go and when to make turns until you reach your destination.
- **Google Lens:** Google Lens initially is an application that allows you to search Google by images; it evolved later to allow object recognition and now it even includes AR part. The AR is used in phone applications (iOS, Android) to do real-time translations of boards, signs, etc. It combines AI to recognize the texts from images and translate them and AR to display it in real time to users [12].

On other hand, ***virtual reality*** is the experience conducted in a completely virtual environment. VR headsets are used to create a simulated environment and help individuals to immerse into it to experience an entirely different reality. Since it is completely virtual, the user is isolated from the real world, and VR cannot be used unless the user has the headset or VR glasses, as these are considered the entry keys to this virtual world. VR is famous in the gaming industry, which creates a virtual world for gamers with virtual characters, a strong story, music and attractive environment design. Gamers like to be fully engaged in the games they play and dislike being distracted; thus, VR is the magical solution that lets them immerse themselves in their games and fully enjoy them. It is also used in the education field to provide knowledge in an appealing manner to students. Few examples of VR products oculus quest Nintendo, Sony PlayStation VR, Lenovo Mirage. Some of the VR applications in real life are:

- **ClassVR:** It is a new concept in the education sector which uses VR to raise engagement and knowledge retention for students. A VR headset is used, equipped with a user-friendly interface, gesture control and embedded educational resources.
- **Meta Horizon Worlds:** Meta Horizon Worlds is an online virtual reality game developed and published by Meta Platforms. On this multiplayer virtual platform, players move and interact with each other in various worlds that host events, games and social activities.

Finally, **Mixed reality** merges the user's physical environment and digitally created content, where both environments can coexist and interact with each other [9]. It mixes between virtual reality and the AR. To use the MR applications, the use of headset or glasses is mandatory; yet, instead of isolating you from the real world like VR, it extends your virtual world with your real surroundings – for example, you may see your virtual characters

TABLE 1.1 AR vs MR vs VR key differentiating features summarized.

FEATURE	AUGMENTED REALITY	MIXED REALITY	VIRTUAL REALITY
Environment	Real-world environment	Real-world and virtual environment blend	Fully immersive virtual environment
Interaction	Interaction with both real and virtual objects	Interaction with both real and virtual objects	Interaction limited to virtual environment
Transparency	Partially transparent, overlays digital content onto real world	Virtual objects appear anchored in real world	Fully immersive, no view of real world
Immersion	Less immersive than VR	Varies from partial to full immersion	Fully immersive
Applications	Education, training, gaming, navigation	Training, design, gaming, entertainment	Gaming, simulations, virtual experiences
Examples	Pokémon Go, Snapchat filters, Heads-up displays (HUDs)	Microsoft HoloLens, Magic Leap, Google Glass	Oculus Rift, HTC Vive, PlayStation VR

from your favorite game roaming your room and sitting on your rolling chair. The best example of it in real life is Microsoft HoloLens, an untethered MR headset that's designed to help you solve real business problems today using intelligent apps [13]. Table 1.1 resumes the key differences between these concepts in terms of their functioning environment, the interaction nature you can have while using these apps, the transparency level to the real world, level of immersion of users, type of applications and popular applications.

1.5 FUTURE TRENDS

The future of AR promises different possibilities and trends that are to define its evolving and adoption. Some of the key future trends of AR are:

- **Widespread across fields of industry:** One of the expected things about AR is that it will be integrated into various sectors beyond what already exists.

- **Suitable wearable devices:** More advanced AR wearable devices are to be created, such as smart glasses and AR headsets as we recently noticed the release of Apple Vision Pro, which is heavy although it gives a great experience; lighter versions are anticipated to be released.
- **3D mapping and spatial computing:** Advancements in spatial computing and 3D mapping technology are expected with better engagement with the real world, resulting in more realistic and precise AR experiences with accurate object detection and interactive physical surface.
- **AR cloud:** One of AR challenges is the complexity of crafting and disseminating AR content, beyond the known constraints such as sluggish mobile data speeds and device capabilities. AR cloud aims to make AR more accessible to a broader audience. AR Cloud is a virtual replica of the real world that provides developers with a foundation to make AR experiences without starting from scratch. For example, while walking on the street, you can use your smartphone camera to observe your environment. An AR application like Google Lens could then employ digital overlays to facilitate targeted searches, display information about nearby businesses, and offer crowdsourced insights like restaurant reviews [14].
- **Social AR Experiences:** AR may be widely be used to enrich social communications. Social media platforms and messaging apps may include AR features, allowing users to share AR stickers, filters and realistic-looking avatars in their conversations and posts, which enables more natural AR experiences.
- **Integration with AI and IoT:** AR applications could be empowered by AI and IoT to enhance their capabilities. Through AI algorithms, AR experiences will become more intelligent and context-aware, while IoT devices provide real-time data to enrich the user's interaction with their environment.
- **AR in Autonomous Vehicles:** AR interfaces may elevate the driving experience by offering navigation guidance and displaying real-time information about road conditions, potential congestion and ideal shortcuts.

REFERENCES

1. Peddie, Jon, *Augmented Reality Where We All Live*, Springer International Publishing, 2017.

2. Ronald, T. Azuma, "A survey of augmented reality," *Presence: Teleoperators and Virtual Environments*, vol. 6, no. 4, pp. 355–385, August 1997.
3. Mathias, Mohring; Christian, Lessig; Oliver, Bimber, "Video See-Through AR on Consumer Cell-Phones," in *Third IEEE and ACM International Symposium on Mixed and Augmented Reality*, Arlington, VA, USA, 2004.
4. Seppala, Timothy J., "Audi's eKurzinfo app uses augmented reality to sidestep A3 owner's manual," En gadget, 12 August 2013. [Online]. Available: https://www.engadget.com/2013-08-12-audi-a3-ekurzinfo-ar-app.html. [Accessed 17 March 2024].
5. A. Inc., "Apple Vision Pro," Apple. [Online]. Available: https://www.apple.com/newsroom/topics/apple-vision-pro/. [Accessed 17 March 2024].
6. "Step-By-Step Guide to Mercedes-Benz Augmented Reality Technology," mbscottsdale, 12 February 2022. [Online]. Available: https://www.mbscottsdale.com/blog/how-to-use-mercedes-benz-augmented-reality-navigation/. [Accessed 17 March 2024].
7. Lardinois, Frederic, "Google Maps gets improved Live View AR directions," 1 October 2020. [Online]. Available: https://techcrunch.com/2020/10/01/google-maps-gets-improved-live-view-ar-directions/. [Accessed 1 May 2024].
8. Naudus, Kris, "'Pokémon Go' is the 'aha' moment AR has been waiting for," 12 July 2016. [Online]. Available: https://www.engadget.com/2016-07-12-pokemon-go-augmented-reality.html?guccounter=1&guce_referrer=aHR0cHM6Ly93d3cuZ29vZ2xlLmNvbS8&guce_referrer_sig=AQAAAKBh2J6_FeFtrA_AIdhqm3iWeOgkBsqdoU67FktmJY9htcmBrkJhaIn0RPcwWau9e-fOWF1mwSl9Iaj1qwpnxDd-eGMHBfM_8hOTkYVg. [Accessed 1 May 2024].
9. Technologies, U., "What is AR, VR, MR, XR, 360?," Unity. [Online]. Available: https://unity.com/how-to/xr-glossary. [Accessed 17 March 2024].
10. "Pokemon Go Statistics," [Online]. Available: https://www.businessofapps.com/data/pokemon-go-statistics/. [Accessed 13 April 2024].
11. Newsroom, I. I., "IKEA Place app launched to help people virtually place furniture at home," IKEA, 12 September 2017. [Online]. Available: https://www.ikea.com/global/en/newsroom/innovation/ikea-launches-ikea-place-a-new-app-that-allows-people-to-virtually-place-furniture-in-their-home-170912/. [Accessed 9 April 2024].
12. Li, Abner, "Google Lens translate camera," 5 December 2022. [Online]. Available: https://9to5google.com/2022/12/05/google-lens-translate-camera/. [Accessed 13 April 2024].
13. "Microsoft HoloLens," Microsoft. [Online]. Available: https://www.microsoft.com/en-us/hololens. [Accessed 9 April 2024].
14. Verizon, "What is the AR cloud and what is it used for?," Verizon, 11 April 2022. [Online]. Available: https://www.verizon.com/about/blog/what-is-ar-cloud. [Accessed 22 March 2024].

Artificial Intelligence

2

2.1 INTRODUCTION

Intelligence is one of the key distinguishing features of humans. The ability to think and analyze using intellect has long characterized the human from other creatures. Intelligence is biologically tied to the brain; however, animals also have brains, but they are unable to think, and they rely mainly on their instincts to survive.

Multiple definitions exist for intelligence, such as being a mental quality consisting of learning from experience, understanding abstract concepts, adapting to situations, using gained knowledge to handle, control and influence the surrounding environment [1]. Another definition is that it is the ability to learn from experience, to adapt, select and shape the environment. Or that intelligence is the generic and specific abilities to intellectual tasks [2].

Another definition states that general intelligence is a mental ability that enables multiple skills, including verbal, numerical, mechanical and spatial [3]. Scientists have long dreamed of making machines that can think; they tried to mimic the way human brain functions and worked toward creating artificial intelligence (AI). In this chapter, we explain AI and its subfield and concentrate more on computer vision and more particularly object detection techniques.

2.2 ARTIFICIAL INTELLIGENCE DEFINITION

AI has been trending with its various applications and the advances it has brought. However, although this concept is popular, it is not new. Theories about AI date back to 1943 when neurophysiologist Warren McCulloch and

DOI: 10.1201/9781042003860-3

logician Walter Pitts investigated the possibility of representing logical functions via networks of artificial neurons. AI is human made inspired by brain functioning created by God; thus, it is coined as artificial. Many scientists explored the concept of machine intelligence that can enable machines to think. However, the term AI as it is known now was coined in 1956 at the Dartmouth Conference by John McCarthy [4]. AI mimics the functioning of the human brain and attempts to make machines that are able to see, learn, reason and act like humans. Under its umbrella, multiple subfields exist such as robotics, machine learning (ML), deep learning (DL), computer vision, natural language processing, etc.

2.3 ARTIFICIAL INTELLIGENCE TYPES

AI is classified into three main categories: the **narrow**, the **general** and the **super AI.**

- The **narrow intelligence** performs specific tasks and cannot generalize broadly beyond its initial task.
- The **general intelligence** is to simulate human intelligence and achieve what humans can do from intellectual activities such as learning, reasoning, problem solving, strategizing and decision-making.
- The **super AI** enables the creation of machines that outsmart human beings [5, 6].

All what is being developed currently of AI applications belongs to the narrow intelligence, the general and super intelligence are currently out of reach.

Another refined classification categorizes AI into four types based on their stage of evolution, the *reactive machine*, the *limited memory*, the *theory of mind* and the *self-aware.*

- The **reactive machines** have no memory or prior event knowledge; they only react when a specific event occurs. Because they are task specific, one of their earliest and most famous applications was in chess-playing computers, such as IBM's Deep Blue.
- **Limited memory machines** have limited memory and interaction with the world; they can learn from past knowledge. One of its applications is autonomous driving cars.

- **Theories of mind** are an advanced type of AI that still does not exist currently; it defines machines that are able to create representations of the world and understand its entities. Some define this as enabling machines to understand human emotions, infer their intentions and predict their behavior.
- **Self-aware** machines are empowered with consciousness that enables them to understand themselves; it is the most advanced level of AI that is currently not implemented [6, 7].

2.4 ARTIFICIAL INTELLIGENCE SUB-FIELDS

AI englobes various fields such as ML, DL, computer vision, generative AI and natural language processing. In Figure 2.1, we give function-based classification to the different AI fields; we categorized them into discriminative AI, which is composed of methods for decision, prediction, classification and regression. Generation and interaction AI, which englobes generative AI, language-centric and cognitive AI, agentic AI, etc. The third category is physical and autonomous systems such as robotics, autonomous driving vehicles, etc. It is important to note that this classification is functional rather than exclusive; many AI systems span multiple categories.

Discriminative AI is composed of ML, DL, probabilistic and logic-based AI in addition to search and optimization AI models. ML enables the machine to learn from data without being explicitly programmed. ML models use mathematics and statistical models to predict the output from the given input. ML has five subtypes, which are supervised learning, unsupervised learning, semi-supervised learning, self-supervised and reinforcement learning [8]. In **supervised learning**, the classification or regression models learn from labeled training data. **Unsupervised learning** uses unlabeled data; it is commonly used for clustering analysis and dimensionality reduction. In **semi-supervised** learning, the model learns from labeled and unlabeled data, making it a mix of supervised and unsupervised learning. In **self-supervised learning**, unsupervised learning is used for supervised learning tasks. They do not rely on labeled data; instead they implicitly generate these labels for unstructured data. **Reinforcement learning** relies on the process of rewards to perform actions [9, 10].

Deep learning is in a matter of fact a subtype of ML; it belongs precisely to supervised learning. DL relies on the use of complex neural networks composed of layers as their building blocks; these layers are connected, and in

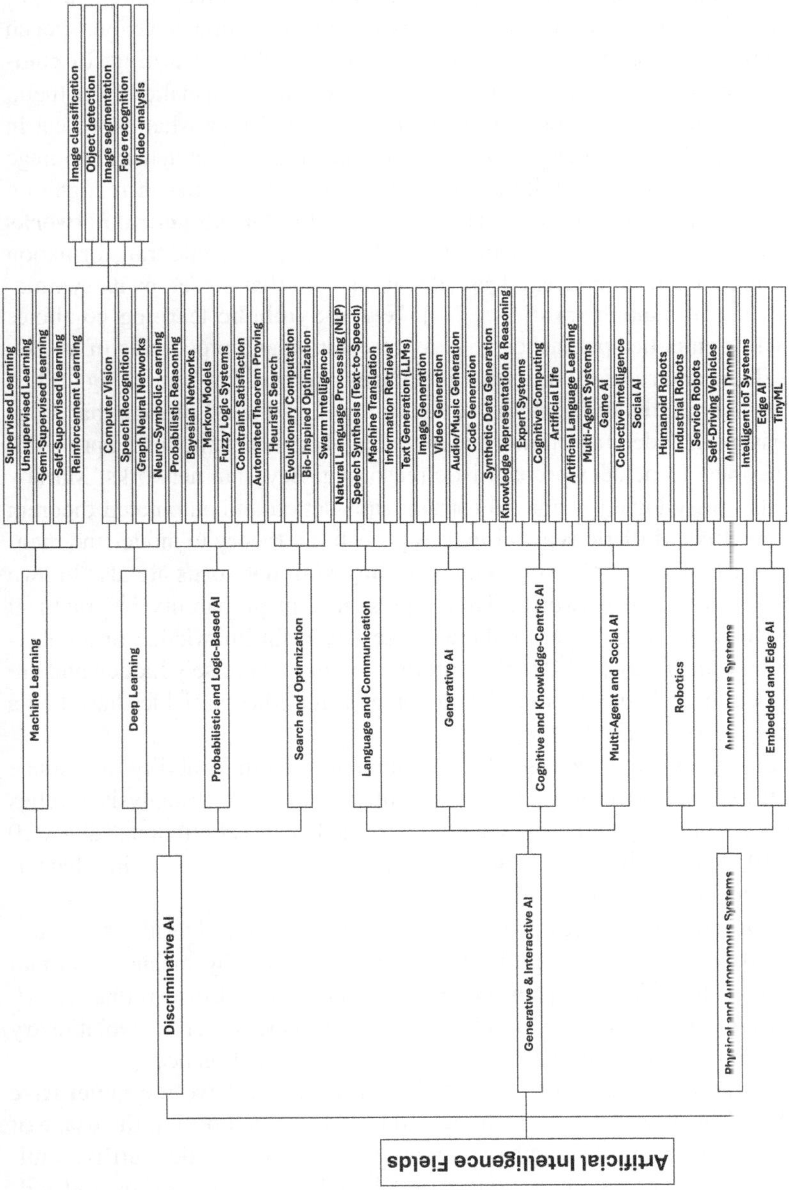

FIGURE 2.1 Artificial intelligence fields.

each layer, multiple nodes exist containing mathematical functions: the first layer in the neural network is the input data and the last is the output (labels). DL has prospered with the emergence of big data [11]. It has multiple usages and applications, which form its subtypes. Mainly, computer vision, speech recognition, graph neural networks and neuro-symbolic learning. In **computer vision**, the computer analyses images to extract information from them, interprets and understands it. It is the use of DL to know what is present in an image and where. It englobes image classification, object detection, image segmentation, face recognition and video analysis [12]. **Speech** recognition uses DL to translate verbal speeches into texts [13]. **Graph neural networks** are used to solve graph prediction tasks. It is an optimizable transformation on graph attributes (nodes, edges, global context) that preserves its symmetries i.e. permutation invariance [14]. **Neuro-Symbolic** learning combines DL with symbolic approaches – i.e. representation and processing of knowledge, logic and rules using formal languages – to perform computing [15].

Probabilistic and logic AI category regroups the AI models that focus on reasoning under uncertainty and modeling this uncertainty using probability theories. It includes probabilistic reasoning, Bayesian networks, Markov models, fuzzy logic systems, constraint satisfaction and automated theorem proving. **Probabilistic reasoning** uses probability theory to model and manage uncertainty in decision-making [16]. **Bayesian networks** are also known as belief or casual networks. They represent joint probability in graphical formalism. They are used to characterize uncertain knowledge in a coherent, convenient way [17]. **Markov models** are more precisely hidden and are statistical models that predict the outcome of unknown variables based on a set of observed variables [18].

Fuzzy logic system resembles the human brain in its ability to produce results and make decisions from approximate knowledge or analysis. It relies on the use of fuzzy logic where a logical variable has a continuous value or 0 or 1 [19]. **Constraint satisfaction** is a flexible approach for searching that has proved its usefulness in AI [20].

Automated theorem proving designs systems and algorithms to automatically validate or contradict mathematical claims by means of formal logic [21]. **Search and optimization** is the last class of discriminative AI, and it regroups the models developed to do heuristic research, evolutionary computation, bio-inspired optimization and swarm intelligence.

In the second category in our classification, we have the **generative models**. These models are the hype and the trend that boosted the usage of AI. From linguistic to security use cases, generative models utilize multiple forms of data such as textual as ChatGPT, images, audios and videos such as synthetic art and deepfakes. In our classification, we divided this class into four sub-categories based on their interaction and generated content. The types are models used for **language and communication**, mainly related to natural language processing models and translation. **Generative AI** can be used to generate text, audio, video, code, or art, etc. **Cognitive and knowledge-centric AI** attempts to mimic human to learn and understand. It includes expert systems, cognitive computing, etc. **Multi-agent and social AI** regroup models used for gaming, collective and social models.

The third category is for **physical and autonomous systems** such as **robots** with all their types and purposes, and **autonomous systems** such as autonomous vehicles and drones. Finally, the **embedded and edge AI** regrouping lightweight models that can run on resource-restricted devices.

2.5 OBJECT DETECTION

Object detection is one of the DL applications, more specifically, one of the computer vision pillar fields. It aims to localize and identify an object in an image or video. It groups two tasks, namely, object localization and object classification. The first is related to finding the location of the object in the image or video and bounding it with a box. The second determines the category to which the object belongs.

The object detection models are trained on labeled data that bound the labeled objects in boxes. A single image may contain multiple objects. Multiple DL models exist such as the You Only Look Once (YOLO) family, Convolutional Neural Network (CNN) and Region-Based Convolutional Neural Network (R-CNN). Object detection has multiple use cases in the real world such as in autonomous driving, the medical field, and physical security to prevent crimes and localize criminals [22].

2.6 YOLOV8 MODEL

YOLO is a family of compound-scaled object detection, image segmentation, and vision AI task models launched by Ultralytics and trained on multiple datasets such as the COCO2017 dataset. It exports to ONNX, CoreML and TFLite [23]. The eighth version of YOLO has a higher mean Average Precision (mAP) and faster inference time than previous versions. YOLOv8 has five pretrained models (n, s, m, l, x). For our experimentation, we used

YOLOv8s for its lightness and fast inference; it is worth mentioning that at the time of writing this book, YOLOv11 is released, but we did not try it, yet.

YOLOv8 model architecture consists of a backbone, neck and head. The backbone is composed of the Cross Stage Partial (CSP) architecture, which splits the feature map into two parts with convolution operations and concatenation. Additionally, it incorporates the C2f module, consisting of two ConvModules (Conv-BN-SiLU) and n DarknetBottleNecks connected through Split and Concat. The model also reduces the number of blocks to 3, 6, 6, 3 across four stages and includes the Spatial Pyramid Pooling – Fast (SPPF) module in Stage 4 to enhance inference speed. The backbone's role is to improve learning ability and reduce computational cost.

In the Neck section, in general, deeper neural networks capture more feature information, enhancing dense prediction quality. However, excessive depth reduces object localization accuracy, and information loss from excessive convolution operations will affect smaller objects. To mitigate this, architectures like Feature Pyramid Network (FPN) and Path Aggregation Network (PAN) are essential for multi-scale feature fusion.

The Head section is composed of a decoupled head, where the classification and detection heads are separated, unlike the coupled head in YOLOv5. The model retains only the classification and regression branches, deleting the objectiveness branch. Additionally, it employs an anchor-free approach, identifying the center of the object and estimating the distance to the bounding box, rather than using numerous anchors to determine offsets. Its role is to enhance object detection accuracy by separating tasks [24].

This enhanced model architecture and optimized algorithms and backbone network contribute to quicker and more efficient object detection. Enabling YOLOv8 to process a higher number of frames per unit of time, making it highly suitable for real-time applications. Additionally, the mAP scores of YOLOv8 have shown improvement compared to YOLOv3b7.

2.7 CONCLUSION

In this chapter, we have briefly described the AI and its fields. In addition to explaining object detection in general and the architecture of the model (YOLOV8), we used in our proof-of-concept in particular. It is noteworthy that although we are currently living in the golden age of artificial intelligence, the concept itself is quite older. What made artificial intelligence bloom are the advances in computing technologies and the availability of large amounts of data. As it is well known that AI models learn by iterating through a tremendous volume of data, which cannot be achieved efficiently if the technology did not allow it. In the next chapter, we explain steganography techniques and the use of AI and AR to exchange files covertly.

REFERENCES

1. Sternberg, Robert J., "Human intelligence," Britannica, 18 Jul 2025. [Online]. Available: https://www.britannica.com/science/human-intelligence-psychology. [Accessed 20 Aug 2025].
2. Sternberg, Robert J, "Intelligence," *Dialogues Clinical Neuroscience*, vol. 14, no. 1, p. 19–27. doi: 10.31887/DCNS.2012.14.1/rsternberg, 2012.
3. Ruhl, Charlotte, "What Is Intelligence In Psychology," Simply Psychology, 1 February 2024. [Online]. Available: https://www.simplypsychology.org/intelligence.html. [Accessed 21 August 2025].
4. "The History of AI," Avicena, 2024 [Online]. Available: https://avicena.tech/wp-content/uploads/2024/03/The-History-of-AI_Avicena.pdf. [Accessed 13 September 2025].
5. "Artificial Intelligence and Libraries," American University Washington DC, 2025 [Online]. Available: https://subjectguides.library.american.edu/lib-ai. [Accessed 21 September 2025].
6. Lev, Craig; Nicole, Laskowski; Linda, Tucci, "What is AI (Artificial Intelligence)? Definition, Types, Examples & Use Cases," Tech Target, 1 October 2024. [Online]. Available: https://www.techtarget.com/searchenterpriseai/definition/AI-Artificial-Intelligence. [Accessed 22 Sept 2025].
7. "What is Artificial Intelligence (AI)?," Google Cloud. [Online]. Available: https://cloud.google.com/learn/what-is-artificial-intelligence. [Accessed 21 September 2025].
8. China, Chrystal R., "Five machine learning types to know," IBM. [Online]. Available: https://www.ibm.com/think/topics/machine-learning-types. [Accessed 23 January 2026].
9. Raschka, Sebastian, "Machine learning lecture notes," *Department of Statistics*, Madison: University of Wisconsin–Madison, 2019.
10. Bergmann, Dave, "What is self-supervised learning?," IBM. [Online]. Available: https://www.ibm.com/think/topics/self-supervised-learning. [Accessed 24 01 2026].
11. Shlomo, Dubnov; Dongmian, Zou, *Lecture Notes in Deep Learning: Theoretical Insights Into an Artificial Mind*, Singapore: World Scientific Connect, 2026.
12. Fergus, Rob, "Computer Vision – Lecture 1," https://cs.nyu.edu/~fergus/teaching/vision/1_Intro.pdf.

13. "What is speech recognition?," IBM. [Online]. Available: https://www.ibm.com/think/topics/speech-recognition. [Accessed 24 January 2026].
14. Sanchez, Benjamin; Lengeling Reif, Emily; Pearce, Adam; Wiltschko, Alexander B., "A Gentle Introduction to Graph Neural Networks," Distill, 2 Sept 2021. [Online]. Available: https://distill.pub/2021/gnn-intro/. [Accessed 24 January 2026].
15. Massimo, Attoresi, "Neuro-symbolic artificial intelligence," EDPS Europa. [Online]. Available: https://www.edps.europa.eu/data-protection/technology-monitoring/techsonar/neuro-symbolic-artificial-intelligence_en. [Accessed 24 January 2026].
16. "Probabilistic Reasoning in Artificial Intelligence," Geeks for Geeks, 23 August 2025. [Online]. Available: https://www.geeksforgeeks.org/artificial-intelligence/probabilistic-reasoning-in-artificial-intelligence/. [Accessed 25 January 2026].
17. "What are Bayesian Networks?," Bayes fusion, 2025. [Online]. Available: https://www.bayesfusion.com/bayesian-networks/. [Accessed 25 January 2026].
18. Abid, Mamoona, "*Hidden Markov Model*," Islamabad, Pakistan: National Skills University, 2023/2024.
19. Pavithra, V.; Jayalakshmi, V., "Chapter 2 - Smart energy and electric power system: Current trends and new intelligent perspectives and introduction to AI and power system," in *Smart Energy and Electric Power Systems Current Trends and New Intelligent Perspectives*, Elsevier, 2023, pp. 19–36.
20. Donaldson, Toby, "Chapter 6: Constraint Satisfaction Problems," 2019. [Online]. Available: https://www.sfu.ca/~tjd/310summer2019/chp6_csp.html. [Accessed 25 January 2026].
21. "Automated Theorem Proving (ATP)," Emergent Mind, 10 July 2025. [Online]. Available: https://www.emergentmind.com/topics/automated-theorem-proving-atp. [Accessed 26 January 2026].
22. Jacob, Murel; Eda, Kavlakoglu, "Object detection," IBM. [Online]. Available: https://www.ibm.com/think/topics/object-detection. [Accessed 25 January 2026].
23. Ultralytics, "Ultralytics YOLO Docs," Ultralytics. [Online]. Available: https://docs.ultralytics.com/. [Accessed 23 April 2024].
24. Ju, Rui-Yang; Cai, Weiming, "Fracture detection in pediatric wrist trauma X-ray images using YOLOv8 algorithm," *Scientific Reports*, vol. 13. doi: 10.1038/s41598-023-47460-7, 2023.

Steganography 3

3.1 INTRODUCTION

Steganography which means hiding messages within ordinary objects, is an old new concept with a history stretching back to ancient civilizations. It has been evolving with the emergence of technology by changing its techniques and cover objects. Nowadays, in our digital smart era, governed by advanced technologies and artificial intelligence (AI) applications, steganography finds itself at the threshold of new possibilities. Throughout history, steganography has been employed between parties to communicate covertly. From ancient Greece to the Roman Empire, genius methods were invented using everyday objects, preparing the foundation for today's digital steganographic techniques.

Fast forward to the modern age, steganography uses digital files such as image, audio, video files and even text documents as carriers for hidden messages in the form of digital files offering fertile ground for covert communication. Nonetheless, it is the evolution of AI that opened new horizons for steganography. Not only did it offer more possibilities for improving the concealment of information – with algorithms refining the embedding process to ensure higher embedded data and securer covertness – but also made more sophisticated steganalysis tools, capable of detecting even the well-hidden messages.

In this chapter, we provide an in-depth exploration of steganography, tracing its historical roots, examining its modern mediums, studying its use cases and applications, and shedding light on the integration of AI for steganography.

3.2 STEGANOGRAPHY HISTORY

Steganography which means "covered writing" is originally Greek term composed of **stegano**, which means hidden and **graphy** standing for writing [1].

DOI: 10.1201/9781042003860-4

Although it has the same purpose as cryptography, which is to transmit messages secretly, it differs from it by the fact that it hides the existence of the message and sends it through implicit means, while the latter sends it explicitly but in an unreadable manner.

To explain it with an easier example, suppose that you are using a paper and pen to send a secret message to your friend; if you hide the message in a particular drawing or write it with invisible ink, you have used steganography to covertly exchange it. But if we suppose that you and your colleague have priorly agreed on a certain code to use and when you use that coding mechanism to encrypt your message hi into (7H), that is cryptography. Your other colleagues may see the code but will not be able to decode the message, while in steganography, they will not even notice the message.

In history, this was known as the prisoner's problem where two prisoners wanted to plan their escape from prison despite being monitored by the guardian. They used a secret method to exchange messages to remain undetectable so that potential monitors do not suspect that they are planning their escape [2].

In ancient times, the Greek historian Herodotus described how ancient Greeks used to shave slaves' heads, tattoo messages onto their scalps and send them as messengers when their hair grew back, effectively hiding the message until its intended recipient revealed it [3]. In addition to tattooing messages onto shaved heads, another technique of steganography consisted of scratching messages onto wooden tablets and then waxing them. The recipient, upon receiving the tablet, would then remove the wax to reveal the hidden message underneath. This method provided a discreet means of communication, as the message remained secret until intentionally uncovered by the recipient. The Romans employed similar methods too.

The Chinese during the Yuan dynasty found a clever way to resist Mongolian rule through steganography. The leaders of that time were unhappy at being obliged to submit to foreign rules; thus, they created a way to coordinating a rebellion without arousing suspicion. Knowing that the moon festival was approaching, they ordered the making of special cakes called "moon cakes"; hidden inside each cake was a message with the outline of the attack. On the night of the festival, the cakes were distributed, the messages were received and the rebels successfully attacked the Mongolian government. What followed was the establishment of the Ming dynasty. Nowadays, moon cakes are eaten to commemorate this legend [4]. The use of these varied techniques demonstrates that ancient civilizations were creative, genius and full of resources in developing secret communication methods for various purposes, including military strategies, espionage and diplomatic correspondence.

During WWII, steganography was a crucial tool in hiding sensitive information. Various techniques were employed to hide messages from prying eyes. Microdots, for example, reduced documents to tiny dots barely visible to the naked eye yet containing valuable intelligence when magnified. Invisible inks provided another means of covert exchange of information, using substances that can only be revealed under specific conditions. Even innocuous items like knitting patterns served as a way for conveying vital information to operatives in the field [5].

These stories from history emphasize that the desire for secrecy and the quest for knowledge are timeless pursuits, woven in human history. From the streets of Rome to the fields of battle, steganography was not just a means of communication; it was a weapon as well, wielded by those who understood the power of information in a world where secrets could change the course of history.

Moving to the modern era, where the digital revolution has transformed communication. Steganography has transitioned into the digital world, finding new applications in the age of technology. Digital steganography involves hiding messages within digital media formats such as images, audio files and video files. In addition to its traditional roles in espionage and military communications, it now serves diverse other purposes. For example, it is used in digital watermarking to protect intellectual property and enforce copyright laws.

3.3 MODERN STEGANOGRAPHY

Nowadays, steganography has taken on new forms. Sending an ordinary photo to a friend may have another purpose than innocently exchanging updates. A Photo may embed a secret message within it that could contain any information. Similarly, trending songs that are listened to by everyone may include more than just a melody and lyrics; while you and others are obsessed with its rhythms, it may carry a hidden message that only intended parties know about and can extract. Even text documents or network traffic can be used to conceal messages in plain sight.

Social media platforms are also a place where steganography can be used. Picture-sharing sites, comment sections and even hashtags can be used as covert channels for communication. Cryptocurrencies, with their decentralized nature, offer yet another avenue for steganographic communication. Within the blockchain transactions are hidden messages, exchanged without the need for a central authority.

Videos offer a larger data capacity compared to images or audio files, making them suitable for hiding larger messages. Steganographic techniques for videos include concealing data within frames or modifying specific aspects of the video encoding process. Even text documents can be used by employing techniques such as whitespace manipulation, font manipulation, or modifying the spacing between letters and words.

Network traffic can be a medium for steganographic communication. Network steganography involves embedding secret messages within network packets or protocols. Imagine sending an email or browsing the web, unaware that inside the packets of data traversing the network lies a hidden message. One method involves modifying the timing or size of network packets to encode information. Another technique is payload-based steganography, where data is embedded within the payload of network packets. By altering the contents of packets or inserting additional data, a covert message can be transmitted alongside legitimate network traffic.

These methods demonstrate that even the most normal activities, such as sending an email or browsing a website, can become means for covert communication. Thanks to the ubiquity of digital communication, network steganography offers a powerful tool for embedding information in real time.

3.4 STEGANOGRAPHY USE CASES AND APPLICATIONS

Steganography applications extend across different fields where secrecy and security are essential. In the world of espionage, where every word can be a matter of life or death, steganography provides invisibility for these words. A picture or an innocent-looking audio file – each can carry hidden secrets embedded within its pixels or sound waves. These covert messages, undetectable to the eye/ear, hold crucial information that could change the course of history. It enables military and intelligence agencies to operate with stealth and precision in digital warfare. Industrial espionage is no exception; there, steganography is used to protect industrial secrets such as designs, procedures, or systems.

Digital watermarking is another application of steganography serving to protecting intellectual rights like how artists sign their works. A watermark can be visible on the work like having a logo imprinted in images, videos, or adding the artist's name within the audios. It can also be invisible, like a digital fingerprint, uniquely identifying the work that can be detected using specific tools; this is similar to copyright infringement online detection when you post an audio file without buying its royalties. The website you are uploading the file to can automatically detect the presence of copyrighted content.

Being frightened by the fact that criminals can use steganography to covertly exchange messages and/or to hide their cyber and physical activities/crimes, steganalysis tools are developed to be employed by forensic investigators to uncover evidence of wrongdoing and bring criminals to justice. By analyzing the digital fingerprints embedded within digital files, investigators can disclose the secrets put within, revealing criminal activities and illicit operations.

Steganography can be used to hide metadata within digital files. Metadata is the silent companion that provides context and information about the content it comes with. It can contain geotagging information – coordinates that pinpoint the exact location where the photo was taken; it is like adding a digital GPS tag to your memories. Similarly, in documents and electronic files, it can embed timestamps, authorship details, or other data to provide context and traceability; it is like leaving a digital footprint, marking each file with a timestamp that records when it was created or modified, or attributing authorship to the person responsible for its creation.

Steganography could be used jointly with cryptography. Cryptography encodes the message, and steganography covers it within innocent-looking digital objects. By combining cryptography with steganography, we create a double layer of security that makes it exponentially more challenging for adversaries to intercept or decrypt the message. It is a powerful strategy that ensures your sensitive information remains safe and secure, even in the face of determined adversaries [6].

3.5 IMAGE AND VIDEO STEGANOGRAPHY TECHNIQUES

Image and video steganography techniques involve hiding secret information within images or video files [7]. These techniques use the characteristics of visual media to cover data in a way that is undetectable by the human eye (see Figure 3.1). Some of these techniques are:

- **Least Significant Bit (LSB) substitution** is one of the most used techniques in image steganography due to its simplicity. It belongs to spatial domain techniques that consists of operating directly on the pixel values of the image to embed the secret message without affecting its visual physical properties. Since the alterations

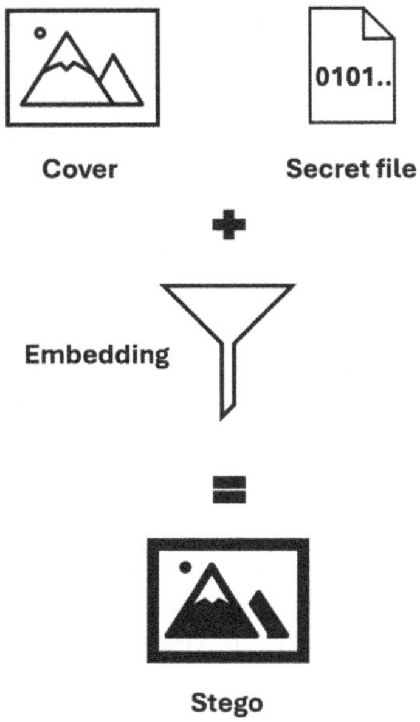

FIGURE 3.1 Traditional Steganography.

are made to the least significant bits, they are imperceptible to the human eye; thus, the resulting stego image appears visually identical to the original cover image. Yet, the embedded message remains encoded within the image data, accessible only to those with the knowledge of the substitution pattern and the ability to extract the embedded information.

- It is noteworthy to mention that this technique is not resilient to image processing such as compression, applying filters and/or cropping the image, because these processes delete the embedded data. An illustration of LSB insertion [8] is given in Figure 3.2. The algorithm is illustrated in Table 3.1.
- **Palette-based techniques** manipulate the images to embed hidden information. This could involve rearranging the colors in the palette, altering their shades and saturation levels, or modifying the color indices themselves to encode the secret message. A color palette is

FIGURE 3.2 Primary LSB insertion.

TABLE 3.1 Steganography by LSB [11]

The hiding algorithm

Input: the cover image (C) and a secret message (m) to hide.
Output: stego image (S)
for i = 1 to l(c) do
$S_i \leftarrow C_i$ /* Creation of the stego file*/
end for
for i = 1 to l(m) do
calculate the index j_i where to save the ith bit of the message
$Sj_i \leftarrow Cj_i \rightleftharpoons mi$
end for

The extraction algorithm

for i = 1 to l(m) do
calculate the index ji where the ith bit of the message is saved
$m_i \leftarrow LSB(Sj_i)$
end for

created from an image and then sorted based on the illumination values of the pixels. The palette is scanned for embedding the secret bit, and the palette index is modified based on the secret bit's value [9].

- **Transform and wavelet domain techniques:** "Transform domain" techniques have an advantage over "spatial domain" techniques because they hide information in areas that are least exposed to image compression, cropping and processing which are, as we mentioned earlier, the disadvantages of spatial domain techniques such as LSB. Some transform domain techniques work independently of the image format, and they can outperform lossless and lossy format conversions [8].
- Discrete cosines transform (DCT) is one of the domain transform techniques which changes the spatial domain image to the frequency domain. It separates the image into spectral sub-bands while respecting its visual quality, i.e. high, medium and low frequency components. In DCT-based steganography techniques, DCT coefficients of the carrier image are obtained. The secret data is inserted into the carrier image for DCT coefficients lower than a certain threshold value (see Table 3.2). To avoid any visual distortion, the integration of secret data is avoided for DCT coefficient values equal to 0 [10].

Another technique of transform domain is discrete wavelet transform (DWT). Wavelets are special functions which (in a form analogous to sine and cosine in Fourier analysis) are used as basic functions to represent signals. The simplest DWT is Haar-DWT. DWT breaks down the image into four

TABLE 3.2 Steganography in DCT [11]

The hiding algorithm
Step 1: Read the cover image. **Step 2:** Read the secret message and convert it to binary. **Step 3:** The cover image is divided into blocks of 8 × 8 pixels. **Step 4:** Scanning the image from left to right, top to bottom, subtract 128 from each block of pixels. **Step 5:** Apply DCT to each block. **Step 6:** Each block is compressed by the quantization matrix. **Step 7:** Read the LSB of each DC coefficient and replace it with a bit of the secret message. **Step 8:** Write the stego image.
The extraction algorithm
Step 1: Read the stego image. **Step 2:** The stego image is divided into 8 × 8 blocks of pixels. **Step 3:** Swiping from left to right, top to bottom subtract 128 in each block of pixels. **Step 4:** Apply DCT to each block. **Step 5:** Each block is compressed by the quantization matrix. **Step 6:** Read the LSB of each DCT coefficient.

sub-section bands: low–low (LL), low–high (LH), high–low (HL) and high–high (HH). LL represents the low-frequency signal, which is the approximation of the original image. LH and HL are intermediate frequency signals; HH is a high frequency signal. LH, HL and HH show changes in information in the image [12]. The LL part contains the most important characteristics. If the information is hidden in this part of the image, it may resist compression and other manipulations. The algorithm is illustrated in Table 3.3 [11].

TABLE 3.3 Steganography in DWT [11]

The hiding algorithm
Step 1: Read the cover image. **Step 2:** Read the secret message and convert it to binary. **Step 3:** Apply DWT and decompose the image into four sub-bands. **Step 4:** Insert the secret message by changing the LSBs of each sub-band **Step 5:** Generate the stego image.
The extraction algorithm
Step 1: Read the stego image. **Step 2:** Calculate the inverse DWT. **Step 3:** Retrieve the message.

TABLE 3.4 Comparison between image steganography techniques [11]

	SPATIAL DOMAIN		*TRANSFORM DOMAIN*	
	LSB	*PALETTE-BASED*	*DCT*	*DWT*
Imperceptibility	High*	High	High	High
Robustness	Weak	High*	High	High
Capacity	High	Weak	Weak	Weak

*: depends on cover image

Let us summarize the information discussed about image steganography in Table 3.4.

We extend the concepts of image steganography to the dynamic video files, where every frame and every pixel can hold secret data.

- **LSB substitution for videos:** Unlike static images, videos offer the ability to hide messages over time. With temporal LSB substitution, the secret message is spread across multiple frames, the hidden information can unfold as the video progresses [13].
- **Motion Vector Modification:** Motion vectors are referred to as digital fingerprints, which comprise the translation of objects between sequential frames. In the video, every frame holds the continuing moving objects in it. Those motion vectors are hidden in each frame as camouflaged arrows that tell the direction and scale of movement for each element. The altering of such vectors, by properly tweaking the direction and velocity, allows us to code a secret message into a video [14].
- Furthermore, the secret message can be embedded in the **sound signal** of the **video**. Voice streams can also be manipulated to hide data by embedding a secret message as signals with an amplitude or frequency that is undetectable to the human ear, and that blends seamlessly with the original soundtrack.

3.6 STEGANOGRAPHY AND AI

AI can help in innovating new steganographic methodologies. For instance, researchers are thinking about using generative adversarial networks (GANs) to tailor cover images adept at hiding secret data [15] or employing natural language processing (NLP) models to embed covert messages within textual content. Some of the works deployed AI techniques for steganography are mentioned in what follows:

Ching-Chun Chang [16] showed how deep neural networks are used to revisit the regular-singular (RS) method and demonstrates its modernization through neuralization. Incorporating adversarial learning helped the RS method to automatically capture the regularity of natural images, replacing handcrafted discrimination functions. Specifically, GANs are trained to predict bit-planes carrying hidden information. A synthetic image generated by GANs guides data embedding and image recovery. The experimental results indicated significant improvements over normal RS implementations.

Hassaballah Mahmoud et al. [17] explained a new method named Harris Hawks optimization-integer wavelet transform (HHO-IWT) for covert communication and secure data transmission within the IoT environment, leveraging digital image steganography. This method hides secret data into cover images using the Harris Hawks optimization (HHO) metaheuristic optimization algorithm, efficiently selecting image pixels for concealing secret bits within integer wavelet transforms.

Xianyi Chen et al. [18] proposed a novel Cover Image Steganography (CIS) approach based on image selection and Star Generative Adversarial Network (StarGAN) to overcome size limitations of existing CIS methods. The secret information is divided into two parts. In the first part, a traditional CIS method based on image mapping and the scale-invariant feature transform (SIFT) feature selects a natural image from a database to the first part of the secret information, while an image mapping is established between the remaining secret information and facial attributes. SIFT algorithm is used to generate robust and distinctive key points and descriptors from images, which can then be hashed to create unique, compact representations for efficient image retrieval, matching and indexing. In the second part, StarGAN generates a high-quality stego image based on the mapping relationship.

Authors of [19] leveraged Deep Convolutional GAN (DCGAN) to embed secret images within other images without altering the image size or raising suspicion. To do so, they used the DCGAN encoder to hide the secret image within a cover image and then used the decoder to extract the secret image from the resulting stego image.

3.7 STEGANOGRAPHY AND AUGMENTED REALITY

Chuanlong Li et al. [20] proposed a novel approach to information hiding using AR combined with deep learning (DL). The proposed AR-based architecture employs a secret-key matching policy where secret messages are mapped to objects, images, or coordinates that act as keys. This approach avoids direct transmission of secret messages and enhances flexibility by using DL models to extend mapping varieties. For example, an image of the Statue of Liberty could represent the Mona Lisa portrait, or a specific coordinate could hide a message.

Another method is the B. Salone's [21], which is a registered patent. It is about making an AR platform with steganography techniques to ensure authorized access. This system consists of a storage device and a processing device that provides an AR application for users to install on their computing devices. The application receives a real-time visual feed with images containing hidden messages. The system verifies if the user's device is authorized to access these messages; if yes, then it generates and overlays an acknowledgment on the visual feed. The system can decrypt the image to reveal the message upon verifying authorization, enhancing secure communication by combining AR and steganography. The system's main applications include determining the real-time status of servers in data centers through embedded messages in server labels.

Ian Maquignaz [22] presents a new PROCAM sensor that employs steganographic techniques to embed invisible patterns in structured light. Allowing a projector to serve dual purposes: as a display device and as a sensor for AR applications. The goal is to develop intelligent projectors that can self-calibrate, interact with users in real-time, and communicate with other devices. The process involves converting input frames into the frequency domain, embedding them with hidden patterns, then projecting and recapturing these frames through the PROCAM system. By filtering the images in the frequency domain, the system decodes the patterns to estimate transformations or extract embedded data. This technique is expected to advance PROCAM AR calibration, steganographic communication and AR systems capable of environment sensing and responsive user interfaces, such as behavior recognition. The results indicate that the system can embed patterns with minimal impact on the original image and reliably extract these patterns with low noise.

3.8 CONCLUSION

In conclusion, steganography is a timeless art form and science that persists and adapts across civilizations and technological epochs that makes us understand that the essence of embedding information within innocuous objects remains as relevant as ever. Applications of steganography are multidisciplinary, from military operations to digital forensics, from copyright protection and privacy preservation to secrecy insurance. Steganography's versatility as a tool for covert communication and data security highlights its significance in an era defined by information exchange and digital connectivity. Moreover, the integration of AI introduced new concepts, presenting opportunities for innovation and challenges for detection. In the next chapter, we explain cryptography techniques thataim to protect information by rendering it unreadable.

REFERENCES

1. Sajedi, Hedieh, *Recent Advances in Steganography*, IntechOpen, 2012.
2. Jessica, Fridrich, *Steganography in Digital Media*, Cambridge University Press, 2010.
3. Backdoor, Quantum, "What Is Steganography?," Medium, 7 September 2020. [Online]. Available: https://medium.com/@.Qubit/what-is-steganography-92c9a611456b. [Accessed 30 April 2024].
4. Kleiman, Dave, *The Official CHFI Study Guide (Exam 312-49): For Computer Hacking Forensic Investigator*, Elsevier Science, 2011.
5. Arpit, Bhayani, "Everything that you need to know about Image Steganography," Medium, 17 January 2020. [Online]. Available: https://medium.com/@arpitbhayani/internals-of-image-steganography-b0d1d60425bf. [Accessed 30 April 2024].
6. Dubey, Richa; Saxena, Apurva; Gond, Sunita, "An innovative data security techniques using cryptography and steganographic techniques," *International Journal of Computer Science and Information Technologies*, pp. 2175–2182, 2015.
7. Li, Li; Zhang, Xinpeng; Chen, Kejiang; Feng, Guorui; Wu, Deyang; Zhang, Weiming, "Image steganography and style transformation based on generative adversarial network," *Mathematics*, vol. 12, no. 4, p. 615, 2024.
8. Pramanik, Sabyasachi; Ghonge, Mangesh Manikrao, Ravi, Renjith V.; Cengiz, Korhan eds. *Multidisciplinary Approach to Modern Digital Steganography*, United States: IGI Global, 2021.
9. Patel, Hetal N.; Khant, Dipanjali R.; Prajapati, Darshana, "Design of a color palette based image steganography algorithm for fractal images," in *International Conference on Wireless Communications, Signal Processing and Networking (WiSPNET)*, Chennai, India, 2017.
10. Hardik, Patel; Preeti, Dave, "Steganography technique based on DCT coefficients," *International Journal of Engineering Research and Applications*, vol. 2, no. 11, pp. 713–717, 2012.
11. Leila, Benarous, "Etudes comparatives d'outils de stéganographie et d'outils de stéganalyse: Application aux images et aux vidéos," University of Laghouat, Laghouat, ALGERIA, 2015.
12. Akbar, Maulana; Setiadi, Moses, "Joint method using Akamatsu and discrete wavelet transform for image restoration," *Applied Computing and Informatics*, vol. 19, no. 3–4, pp. 226–238, 2023.

13. BanuPriya, R.; Deepa, J.; Suganthi, S., "Video steganography using LSB algorithm for security application," *International Journal of Mechanical Engineering and Technology*, vol. 10, no. 01, pp. 203–211, 2019.
14. Kasra, Rezagholipour; Mohammad, Eshghi, "Video Steganography Algorithm based on motion vector of moving object," in *Eighth International Conference on Information and Knowledge Technology (IKT)*, Hamedan, Iran, 2016.
15. Zhang, Xinpeng; Chen, Kejiang; Feng, Guorui; Wu, Deyang; Zhang, Weiming, "Image steganography and style transformation based on generative adversarial network," *Mathematics*, vol. 4, no. 615, p. 12, 2024.
16. Chang, Ching-Chun, "Adversarial learning for invertible steganography," *IEEE Access*, vol. 8, pp. 198425–198435, 2020.
17. Mahmoud, Hassaballah; Mohamed, Abdel; Awad, Ismail; Muhammad, Khan, "A novel image steganography method for industrial internet of things security," *IEEE Transactions on Industrial Informatics*, vol. 17, no. 11, pp. 7743–7751, 2021.
18. Chen, Xianyi; Zhang, Zhentian; Qiu, Anqi; Xia, Zhihua; Xiong, Neal N, "Novel coverless steganography method based on image selection and StarGAN," *IEEE Transactions on Network Science and Engineering*, vol. 9, no. 1, pp. 219–230, 2022.
19. Youcef, METABIS, "Sécurité Des Images: Stéganographie et Cryptographie," University of Laghouat, Laghouat, ALGERIA, 2023.
20. Li, Chuanlong; Sun, Xingming; Li, Yuqian, "Information hiding based on augmented reality," *Mathematical Biosciences and Engineering*, vol. 16, no. 5, pp. 4777–4787, 2019.
21. Sloane, B., "System for implementing steganography-based augmented reality platform". United States of America Patent US-11551426-B2, 10 January 2023.
22. Maquignaz, Ian, "*Imperceptible Pattern Embedding: Structured Light Steganography For Augmented Reality Applications*," ProQuest, 2019.

Cryptography 4

4.1 INTRODUCTION

This chapter serves as a foundational exploration of cryptography, a critical discipline within the broader landscape of information security. At its core, cryptography is employed to preserve the confidentiality of sensitive information by transforming it into a format that remains unintelligible to anyone except authorized entities possessing the correct decryption credentials. While it shares the ultimate goal of protection with steganography, the two fields approach security from different angles. Steganography is primarily concerned with concealing the very existence of a message, ensuring that an observer remains unaware that communication is taking place. Cryptography, on the other hand, makes no attempt to hide the presence of data; instead, it renders the content meaningless to unintended observers. Even if an encrypted message is intercepted, the cryptographic transformation ensures that the data appears disordered and indecipherable without the proper key.

The majority of cryptographic techniques rely on the use of secret keys to facilitate this secure exchange. These keys act as the essential variable that locks and unlocks information, forming the basis of trust in digital communications. However, hashing represents a significant exception to this key-dependent paradigm. Hashing algorithms operate without keys and are designed primarily to protect data integrity rather than secrecy. By generating a unique fixed-size string of characters from an input of any size, hash functions allow systems to detect even the slightest alteration to data. Furthermore, these functions are integral components of digital signature schemes. In such systems, hashing is combined with encryption to validate both the authenticity of the sender and the integrity of the message, ensuring that data has not been tampered with during transit.

DOI: 10.1201/9781042003860-5

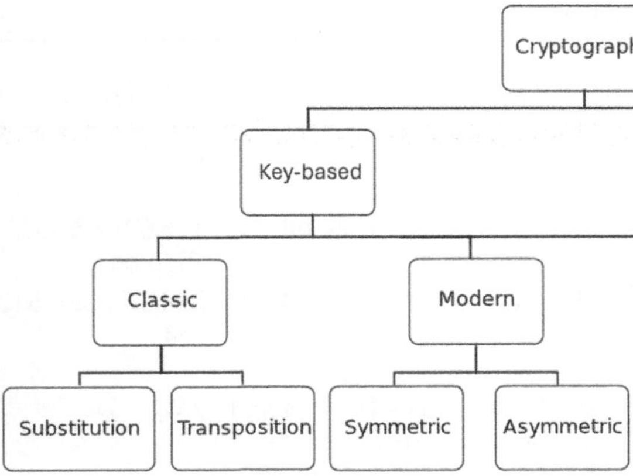

FIGURE 4.1 Classification of key cryptography methods.

As we progress further into the digital age, the security landscape is evolving due to recent advances in quantum computing. This technological shift has prompted the development of quantum-resistant cryptographic schemes, which aim to preserve security even in the presence of quantum adversaries. The urgency of this development arises because quantum computers have the potential to efficiently solve complex mathematical problems, such as integer factorization and discrete logarithms, which currently form the foundation of many conventional cryptographic systems. If left unaddressed, these advancements could render standard encryption methods vulnerable, necessitating a transition to more robust algorithms.

To provide a structured understanding of these concepts, Figure 4.1 illustrates the main categories of cryptographic techniques that will be discussed in the subsequent subsections. This chapter will break down each category, examining their operational mechanisms, their roles in maintaining security, and their relevance to the broader framework proposed in this research. By establishing a clear understanding of these cryptographic primitives, we lay the groundwork for integrating them with steganographic methods in later chapters, ensuring a comprehensive approach to covert communication.

4.2 HASHING

Hashing is a one-way, non-invertible computational process that maps input data of arbitrary length to a fixed-size output of x bits. Numerous hash

TABLE 4.1 Comparison between famous hashing functions [2]

COMPARISON CRITERIA	*MD5*	*SHA-1*	*SHA-2*	*SHA-3*
Year Introduced	1992	1995	2002	2008
Block Size	512 bits	512 bits	512/1024 bits	1152/1088/832/576 bits
Hash Digest Size (Output)	128 bits	160 bits	224/256/384/512 bits	224/256/384/512 bits
Rounds of Operations	64	80 (4 groups of 20 rounds)	64 (SHA-224 and SHA-256) 80 (SHA-384 and SHA-512)	24
Construction	Merkle-Damgård	Merkle-Damgård	Merkle-Damgård	Sponge (Keccak)
Collision Level	High	High	Low	Low
Successful Attacks	Many	Yes	SHA-256 has never been broken	Few collision-type attacks demonstrated
Common Weaknesses	Vulnerable to collisions	Vulnerable to collisions	Susceptible to preimage attacks	Susceptible to practical collision and near-collision attacks
Security Level	Low	Low	High	High
Deprecated	Yes	Yes	No	No

algorithms have been developed for this purpose, including MD5, SHA-1, SHA-2, and SHA-3 (refer to Table 4.1 for a comparison between these hashing functions). Hash functions are widely applied in digital security, particularly for integrity verification in digital signatures and for the secure storage of user passwords. Owing to their computational efficiency and irreversible nature, hash functions are especially suitable for these applications. For example, when a document produces the same hash value as that embedded within a digital signature, it is assumed that the document has not been modified. Likewise, password protection systems do not store plaintext credentials; instead, they store their hash values. During authentication, the hash of the entered password is computed and compared with the stored hash and access is granted only if the two values match.

Both applications fundamentally depend on the assumption of hash uniqueness. Although modern hash functions are designed to minimize collisions, situations in which distinct inputs generate identical hash outputs remain theoretically possible. Such a collision could enable an attacker to authenticate successfully without possessing the original password, provided an alternative input produces the same hash. Similarly, a modified document that results in an identical hash value would incorrectly be deemed unchanged, thereby undermining integrity verification. While identifying such collisions is computationally infeasible for well-designed, low-collision hash functions, the possibility cannot be entirely eliminated at a theoretical level.

In the proof-of-concept implementation presented in Chapter 6, the SHA-256 algorithm was adopted to safely store the passwords. SHA-256 is specifically constructed as a one-way function that transforms input data through a sequence of mathematical operations to generate a distinctive digital fingerprint. This fingerprint uniquely represents the original data, making the recovery of the input from its hash computationally impractical. As a result, even minor alterations to the input data lead to substantially different hash outputs, a property that is essential for reliable integrity verification [1].

4.3 CLASSIC CRYPTOGRAPHY

Traditional cryptography did not incorporate the sophisticated computations or lengthy keys that define contemporary cryptographic schemes. In addition to maintaining the secrecy of the encryption key, the algorithm itself had to remain confidential. In modern contexts, these classical methods are no longer regarded as secure and are largely relegated to educational demonstrations or informal, recreational exchanges. They are particularly susceptible to cryptanalytic approaches such as frequency analysis. Among classical cryptographic techniques, some rely on substituting letters, while others employ transposition, which involves rearranging the positions of letters. Substitution-based ciphers include well-known schemes such as the Caesar cipher, affine cipher, and Vigenère cipher, whereas transposition-focused methods include the Hill cipher. Certain ciphers, like the ADFGX cipher, combine elements of both substitution and transposition, demonstrating a hybrid approach. These examples represent only a small portion of the diverse array of classical cryptographic methods within each category.

4.4 MODERN CRYPTOGRAPHY

With the growing significance of security and its increasingly diverse applications, alongside rapid technological advancements, the demand for more resilient cryptographic solutions tailored to the digital environment emerged. Such solutions must be computationally hard to break, and critically, their security should rely on the secrecy of the keys rather than on concealing the algorithm itself.

4.4.1 Symmetric Cryptography

Symmetric cryptography operates on the principle that the same key is used for both encryption and decryption and that this key must remain confidential. Since only the communicating parties possess the key, ensuring its secure transmission and storage is essential for maintaining secrecy. The general mechanism of symmetric cryptography is illustrated in Figure 4.2. Several well-known symmetric encryption schemes exist, including the Data Encryption Standard (DES), Triple DES (3DES), and the Advanced Encryption Standard (AES). It is worth noting that DES employs a fixed key length of 56 bits, whereas AES supports key lengths of 128, 192, or 256 bits. Similarly, DES operates on 64-bit blocks, while AES uses 128-bit blocks. The number of rounds in DES is constant, whereas in AES, it varies according to the key length. Furthermore, DES and 3DES (TDES) are slower and provide a lower level of security compared to AES. Both are considered deprecated, and AES is now the recommended standard for modern symmetric encryption [3]. Motivated by its security and efficiency, we selected

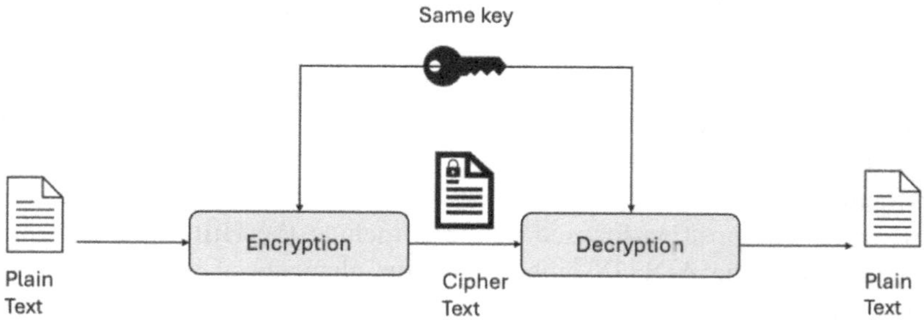

FIGURE 4.2 Symmetric cryptography.

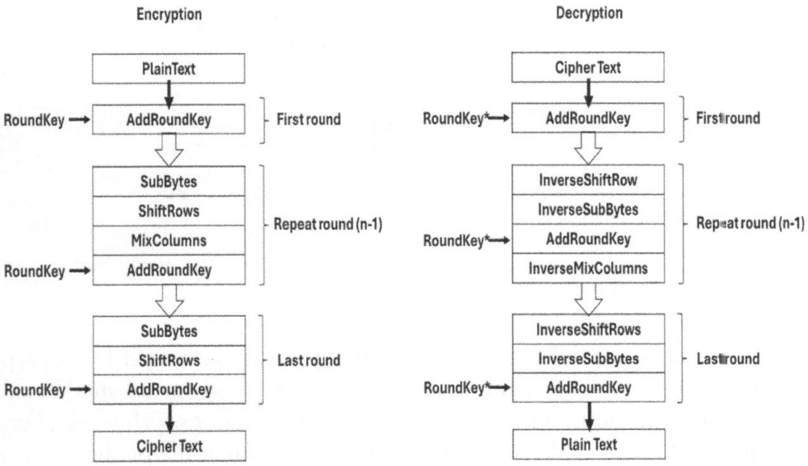

FIGURE 4.3 AES encryption and decryption.

the AES for its in our proof-of-concept implementation, which is explained in the following subsection.

- Advanced Encryption Standard

Rijndael, the original algorithm underlying the Advanced Encryption Standard (AES), is a block cipher that processes data in fixed 128-bit blocks and supports cryptographic keys of 128, 192, or 256 bits. Initially, the plaintext is segmented into 128-bit blocks. A secret key is then used to generate a sequence of distinct round keys, which serve to strengthen the encryption process. Each block of data undergoes multiple rounds of substitution, permutation, and mixing operations using these round keys, ultimately producing the ciphertext. The number of rounds varies according to the key size: ten rounds for a 128-bit key, 12 rounds for a 192-bit key, and 14 rounds for a 256-bit key. During decryption, the ciphertext is transformed back into the original plaintext by applying the inverse operations with the same secret key [4, 5]. The overall AES encryption and decryption procedures are illustrated in Figure 4.3.

4.4.2 Asymmetric Cryptography

While symmetric cryptography is both fast and secure, the challenge of safely distributing the secret key motivated the development of asymmetric cryptographic mechanisms. These systems employ a pair of mathematically linked

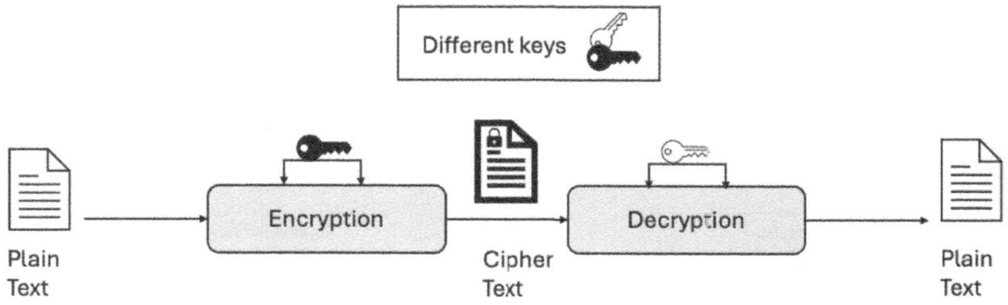

FIGURE 4.4 Asymmetric cryptography.

keys: a public key, used for encryption, and a private key, used for decryption (see Figure 4.4). Asymmetric schemes rely on advanced mathematical concepts, including group theory, algebraic operations, prime numbers, modular arithmetic, and related computations. Although the public key and the encryption/decryption algorithms are publicly known, deriving the corresponding private key is computationally difficult, particularly when long keys are employed. This difficulty arises from problems such as integer factorization in multiplication-based algorithms or the discrete logarithm problem in exponentiation-based schemes. A brute-force attack, which attempts all possible keys, is rendered impractical due to the key length and current technological limitations.

Asymmetric mechanisms are resource-intensive and slower in execution due to the complex mathematical computations involved. Symmetric mechanisms are robust and more lightweight but are generally less secure than their asymmetric counterparts. Consequently, hybrid cryptosystems are now employed, combining both types of mechanisms. In such systems, asymmetric solutions like Rivest–Shamir–Adleman (RSA) are used for the secure exchange of the secret key, while symmetric solutions like AES are used to encrypt the exchanged data.

Asymmetric cryptography supports confidentiality by allowing a message to be encrypted with the recipient's public key and decrypted with the corresponding private key. It also provides authenticity and integrity by enabling the encryption of a message hash with a private key, which can then be verified using the public key (see Figure 4.5). Prominent asymmetric algorithms include RSA and ElGamal. Moreover, the need to securely exchange secret keys led to the development of specialized protocols, such as the public key distribution system, exemplified by the Diffie-Hellman key exchange, which allows parties to establish a shared secret over an insecure channel.

Despite their advantages, asymmetric mechanisms are computationally intensive and slower in execution due to the complex mathematical operations involved. In contrast, symmetric mechanisms are generally

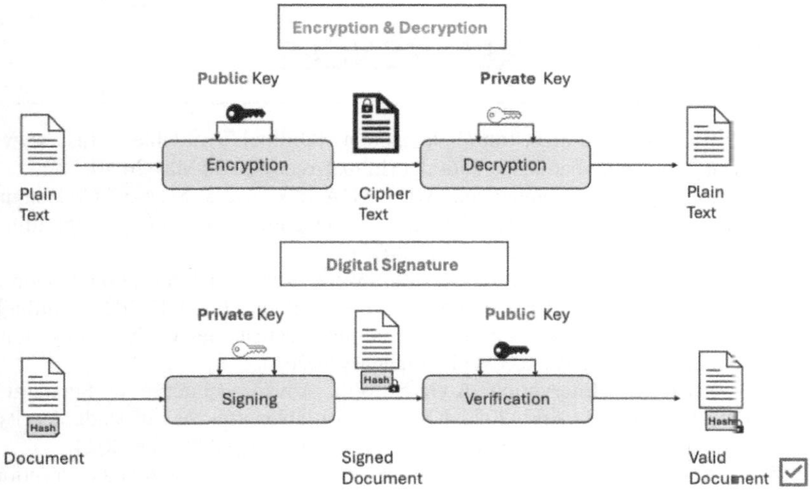

FIGURE 4.5 Public key encryption, decryption and signatures processes.

faster and more lightweight, though they may offer lower security in certain contexts. To leverage the strengths of both approaches, hybrid cryptosystems are now commonly employed. In such systems, asymmetric algorithms like RSA are used to securely exchange the secret key, while symmetric algorithms such as AES handle the encryption of the actual data.

4.5 CONCLUSION

In this chapter, we explained cryptography and how it differs from steganography in its functioning principle. Both cryptography and steganography aim to secure the exchange of secrets, and when used combined, they provide a higher level of security. We presented the two types of modern cryptography, which are symmetric and asymmetric. Additionally, we explained hashing and its uses. In the next chapter, we introduce you to our proposed design for a steganography technique in the era of augmented reality emerging applications, which spread with Meta and Apple Vision. Our proposal mixes AR, AI, and steganography for secret exchange in an innovative way.

REFERENCES

1. “What-is-sha-256-algorithm?,” Javatpoint. [Online]. Available: https://www.javatpoint.com/what-is-sha-256-algorithm. [Accessed 20 May 2024].
2. “Hash Algorithm Comparison: MD5, SHA-1, SHA-2 & SHA-3,” Code signing store. [Online]. Available: https://codesigningstore.com/hash-algorithm-comparison. [Accessed 26 January 2026].
3. precisely, “AES vs DES Encryption: Why Advanced Encryption Standard (AES) has replaced DES, 3DES and TDEA,” Precisely, 14 11 2022. [Online]. Available: https://www.precisely.com/data-security/aes-vs-des-encryption-standard-3des-tdea/. [Accessed 26 January 2026].
4. “What Is AES Encryption? A Guide to the Advanced Encryption Standard,” Panda Security, 14 April 2024. [Online]. Available: https://www.pandasecurity.com/en/mediacenter/what-is-aes-encryption/. [Accessed 20 May 2024].
5. Cam, Hakan; Özduran, Volkan; Ucan, Osman Nuri, “A combined encryption and error correction scheme: AES-turbo,” *Journal of Electrical & Electronics Engineering*, vol. 9, no. 1, 2009.

5 Design of Covert Communication in Meta Era

5.1 INTRODUCTION

Building upon the theoretical foundation established in the preceding chapters, we have examined the core principles, historical evolution and current applications of artificial intelligence (AI), augmented reality (AR), cryptography and steganography. These disciplines, while distinct in their origins, converge to form the backbone of modern immersive technologies. Armed with this comprehensive understanding, we identified a critical opportunity to design a covert communication framework tailored for the emerging "metaverse", a complex digital ecosystem where the physical and virtual worlds coexist and interact dynamically.

Within this immersive landscape, which is primarily driven by mixed reality (MR), virtual reality (VR) and AR applications, security emerges as a paramount concern. The ability to exchange sensitive information covertly in such a multi-layered environment is not only crucial for confidentiality but also inherently challenging. This difficulty stems from the nature of the environment itself; because this world is constructed upon digital infrastructure, it acts as an extension of the traditional cyberworld. Consequently, it inherits the weaknesses and vulnerabilities of conventional networks while simultaneously introducing novel security issues related to spatial computing and virtuality. The blending of physical triggers with digital overlays creates new attack surfaces that traditional security measures often fail to address.

Taking these complexities into consideration, our objective was to engineer a covert communication method specifically operational within an AR context. The proposed mechanism is designed to be triggered by real-world events while concealing the actual secret within the virtual cyber layer, effectively hiding data in plain sight among digital artifacts. To achieve this, we

DOI: 10.1201/9781042003860-6

orchestrated multiple advanced concepts: ensuring the innocuousness of the carrier media, employing robust steganography and encryption standards, leveraging AI for optimization, integrating secret-destruction protocols for ephemeral data security, and anchoring it all within an AR interface.

In this chapter, we move from the conceptual phase to the architectural phase. We explain the design of our framework in an abstract manner, outlining the high-level logic and structural relationships between these components without yet delving into the specific code-level implementation. This abstract design serves as a blueprint, demonstrating how these disparate technologies integrate to form a cohesive, secure and functional system capable of operating within the nuanced security landscape of the metaverse.

5.2 MOTIVATION

The rapid advancement of AR, VR and extended reality (XR) technologies – driven by the widespread adoption of AR applications and games, the growing availability of VR headsets, and major innovations such as the metaverse and Apple Vision – has created new research opportunities, particularly when these technologies are integrated with AI. In our book, we focus on AR due to its extensive user base and high accessibility, primarily through smartphone applications and AR glasses. These characteristics make AR especially attractive for practical deployment and well suited to steganographic applications, which rely fundamentally on the principles of innocence and imperceptibility.

The effectiveness of steganography is strongly influenced by the choice of the cover medium, the data-hiding technique, and the manner in which stego files are exchanged without detection. As such, successful steganographic systems depend on cover media that are both widely used and unlikely to arouse suspicion. Following the global success of Pokémon Go, AR experienced rapid expansion across diverse domains, including education, media and navigation, further reinforcing its suitability as a platform for steganographic communication. Although VR and XR technologies also offer promising potential, their adoption remains comparatively limited due to the high cost of specialized hardware, making AR a more accessible and pervasive alternative.

Figure 5.1 illustrates the AR paradigm and highlights the different methods considered for embedding secret information within this environment. As depicted, AR seamlessly integrates real-world scenes with virtual elements that are perceived through smartphones or AR glasses [1]. These virtual components are activated by real-world cues, such as navigational overlays in Google Maps' Street View mode or virtual characters in location-based games like Pokémon Go.

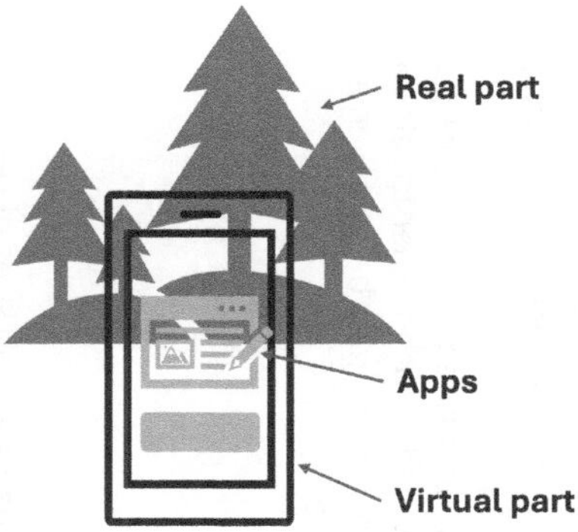

FIGURE 5.1 Augmented reality.

Initially, three principal strategies for integrating steganography with AR were investigated: (1) concealing information within real-world objects, (2) embedding data within virtual elements, and (3) hiding information within the AR application package itself. Table 5.1 presents a comparative evaluation of these approaches, outlining their respective advantages and limitations. Based on this analysis, a hybrid strategy was adopted in our proposed framework which we denote shortly as Stego-AR. In Stego-AR, we combined elements from all three approaches. This integrated solution supports both data embedding and extraction while using virtual objects triggered by real-world cues.

To differentiate our proposed framework from other similar propositions from other researchers which we briefed in Section 3.7, we made a comparison in Table 5.2 highlighting the functioning principle of each solution including ours in addition to their potential vulnerabilities.

5.3 DESIGN OF A COVERT COMMUNICATION METHOD IN META ERA

The main aim of our Stego-AR framework is to offer a secure and dynamic solution for secret exchange. Thus, we designed it to run on mobile application to ensure its ease widespread and usage. The more it is used, the better it is. Our application is designed to have two modes, namely, generic and steganographic.

TABLE 5.1 Potential steganography methods in AR

METHOD	*FUNCTIONALITY*	*ADVANTAGE*	*DISADVANTAGE*
Hiding in the real part	Two main approaches can be used to hide information within real-world elements. The first approach consists of capturing an image of a real-world scene, embedding the secret data into the image, and then transmitting the modified image. The second approach involves storing the captured scene within the application during the data embedding stage and later using the same scene as a trigger for extracting the hidden information.	• Supports the concealment of secret files of varying sizes, ranging from small to large. • Straightforward to implement.	• **First method:** Steganography is applied in a conventional manner, similar to standard image steganography applications, without fully exploiting the capabilities of the AR environment. As a result, the modified image may be intercepted, and the hidden information could be extracted without the need for the AR application. • **Second method:** The user is required to recreate or revisit the same real-world scene in order to retrieve the hidden information, which may be inconvenient and difficult in practice.
Hiding in the virtual part	The secret data is embedded within digital objects or virtual elements that are superimposed onto the real-world scene.	• Secret data is embedded within AR objects. • AR objects are less likely to be suspected as carriers of hidden information.	• Restrictions exist on the types and sizes of secret files that can be embedded. • Implementation in deployed applications is challenging, particularly in defining when and how embedding occurs and determining who can trigger it. • If a secret file is distributed across multiple objects, the sequence of these objects must be carefully tracked.

		• Enables practical exploration of the AR environment for steganographic purposes.	• All users with access to the application may unknowingly possess a copy of the hidden data, increasing the risk of exposure. • This method is generally suitable for one-time use rather than repeated or ongoing scenarios. • Processing of object files during application packaging (e.g., compression) may corrupt or destroy the embedded secret data.
Hiding in the AR app package	The secret file is embedded directly within the application package, either before or after packaging, for example by appending it to the end of the binary or using techniques such as LSB.	• Simple to implement. • Can accommodate secret files of various types and sizes. • Less likely to raise suspicion, particularly when the data is hidden within the application package.	• Like other OS, VR, or mobile application approaches, this method does not fully take advantage of the AR environment. • Embedding the secret within the binary file carries the risk that the data could be corrupted or lost if the application package is compressed during transfer.

TABLE 5.2 Comparison of related works with our proposal

WORK	*FUNCTIONING PRINCIPLE*	*POTENTIAL VULNERABILITY*
Li et al. [2]	In an augmented reality environment, object detection is employed to transmit a secret. Each detected object can represent a specific portion of the secret, and by combining the information from all relevant objects, the complete secret can be reconstructed.	• The choice of objects to be detected, as well as their order, is essential for correctly reconstructing the secret message. If either the objects or their sequence is revealed, the hidden information could be compromised. • There may be restrictions on the size and type of secret data that can be embedded.
Salone et al. [3]	The secret is hidden within real-time visual signals captured from the AR environment. These images are transmitted to the recipient, who can reveal and access the hidden information after successful AR-based authentication on their device.	• The authors did not include detailed implementation information in their paper. • The main approach involves embedding information within images, with its effectiveness depending on the chosen embedding algorithm. Image steganography is also generally vulnerable to image processing operations, such as compression. • Although the authors highlight that only authenticated users can access the secret data, the method remains vulnerable to eavesdropping and interception.
Wilson [4]	The embedded data is stored within files and applications operating in the virtual environment and is exchanged when the virtual application is packaged.	Although the packaged application was resistant to steganalysis, examining the files within the virtual app could still reveal the hidden data, especially if common embedding tools like OurSecret, OpenPuff, or DeepSound were used.

TABLE 5.2 (*Continued*) Comparison of related works with our proposal

WORK	*FUNCTIONING PRINCIPLE*	*POTENTIAL VULNERABILITY*
Our Proposal	Our application combines several advanced technologies, including AR, AI, encryption, image steganography, hashing and secure file destruction. The system's main feature allows users to select a file to hide, which is then embedded into a blank image generated specifically for each session. The image itself is not directly shared; instead, the recipient accesses it through an indirect method. Both the hiding and revealing of the secret file rely on identifying the correct object, or "trigger", using AI-based object detection. Before embedding, the file is encrypted to protect its contents, and the correct decryption key is required to reveal the hidden information. This ensures that only authorized users can access the secret data. Once the secret is displayed in the AR environment, it is immediately destroyed. Both the stego image and the secret file are deleted after being shown, preventing any possibility of replay attacks and maintaining the overall security of the system.	• The security of this application depends on the strength of the cryptography and image steganography methods employed. • If an attacker gains access to the server after the secret has been generated but before it is read by the recipient, they could access the stego file containing the encrypted secret. This file could then be stolen or destroyed. Therefore, it is essential to use a steganography method that is difficult to reverse and a strong cryptography method that cannot be broken within a practical timeframe. • The security of the server must be ensured.

FIGURE 5.2 Our Stego-AR security layers.

Our desire for the widespread related to the generic innocuous mode, the emergence of the application adds a layer of security since not everyone will be using the steganographic mode, it will be difficult to intercept or detect the use of steganographic mode between exchanging parties.

The innocuous mode could be any type of application, it could be a game, an educational program, etc. In our case, we considered in the proof-of-concept an AR-application that displays descriptions about technological gadgets and their functions. The second layer of security is the secret mean to activate the steganographic mode which is known only to those interested to use the application for secret exchange. The third layer is the use of cryptography to encrypt/decrypt the files before their exchange. The fourth layer is the use of steganography to hide the encrypted file triggered by physical object. The fifth layer is the self-destruction property which wipes the file upon its reading by the recipient. Figure 5.2 depicts these layers use in AR environment to achieve the covert file exchange.

Our AR app is a mobile phone with a frontend and a backend. The backend is divided into parts that are executed on the phone and others on the server. The mobile phone AR app hides secret files constrained by real object triggers that are custom trained to detect them. This AR app has two modes briefed in pseudo-Algorithm 1; the first role is a generic role where the camera is used to expand reality with descriptions about the objects it detects. This role is given to normal users; the second role is a steganographic role. It is activated for users aiming to hide and exchange data. It is a secret functionality that our application offers to those interested in security. The user activates the secret functionality and uses the camera to detect an object as the embedding/extraction trigger, then selects the file to exchange, which is encrypted with the passphrase they provide and then hidden. The recipient needs to do similar steps in reverse order: They should activate the secret functionality to be able to unhide a message; then they need to detect the object triggering the hiding process, use the correct password, and view the secret files. For extra security measures, the secret file is destroyed as soon as viewed.

We assume that the sender and the receiver agree thorough other means on the object and the passphrase to use, such as over phone or other means. The mechanism upon which they agree on this information is user dependent and is out of the scope of this discussion. See Figure 5.3 for the visual illustration of the functioning of our Stego-AR app with its two modes.

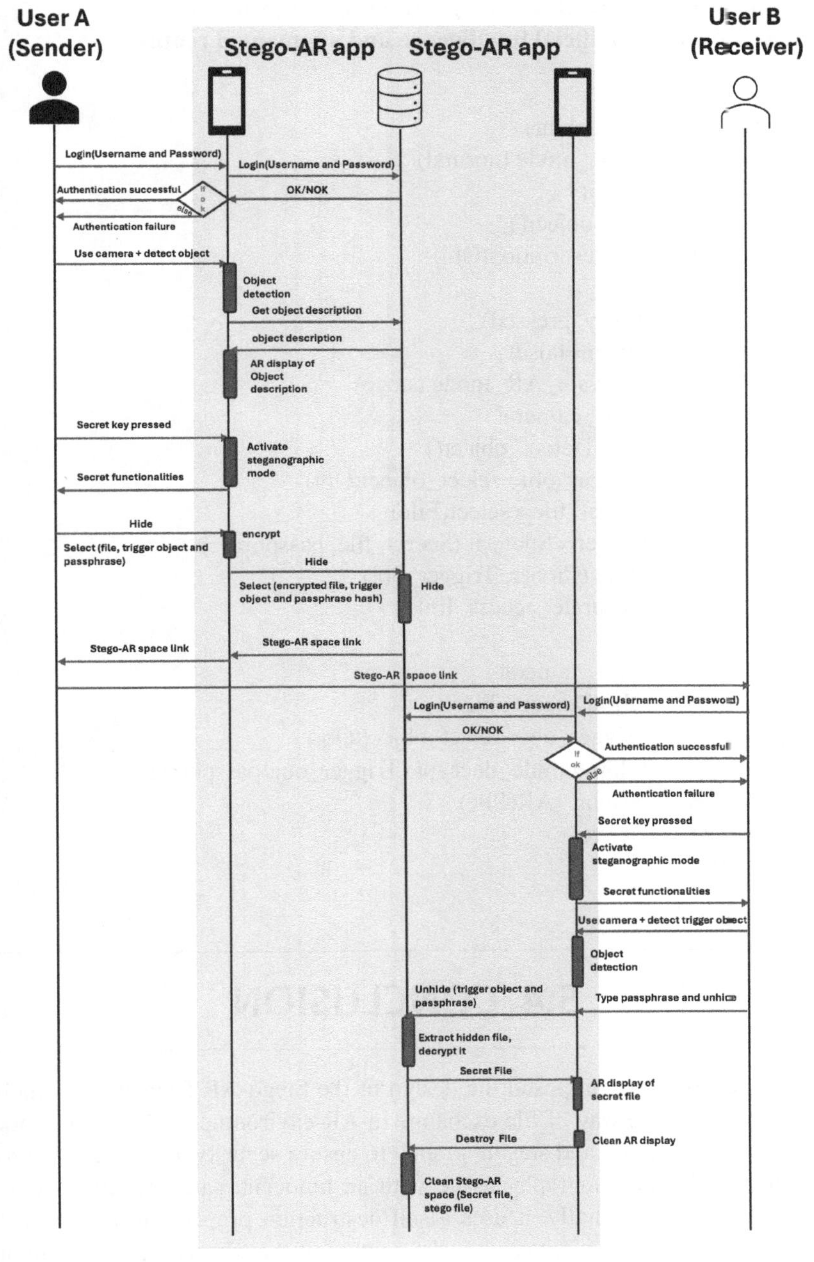

FIGURE 5.3 Visual illustration of the functioning of our Stego-AR app with its two modes.

Algorithm 1: covert file exchange by leveraging encryption, steganography, artificial intelligence and augmented reality

```
Begin
If (user_type=regular)
    Activate_AR_mode (normal)
    Start_camera()
    Obj=Detect_object()
    Show_AR_description(Obj)
Else
    If (secret_key_pressed)
        If (hidden=false)
            Activate_AR_mode (stego)
            Start_camera()
            Obj=Detect_object()
            Trigger_obj= select_object(Obj)
            Secret_file= select(File)
            Cipher= Encrypt (Secret_file, passphrase)
            Hide (Cipher, Trigger_obj)
            Generate_access_link()
        Else
            Start_camera()
            Obj=Detect_object()
            Trigger_obj= select_object(Obj)
            File= unhide_decrypt (Trigger_obj, passphrase)
            Display_AR(File)
            Delete()
End
```

5.4 CONCLUSION

In this chapter, we proposed the design of the Stego-AR framework, which provides a secure way of file exchange in AR environment. Our framework relies on encryption and steganography to ensure security. It also uses AI to obfuscate the steganography usage with an innocent, safe and informative application. Additionally, it uses a self-destruction property to ensure that only the sender and receiver view the content of the file and once viewed, it is deleted. This prevents adversaries from accessing the file later. Our framework is designed to be secure. It is flexible, and it can be improved and varied.

The innocuous application could be any AR app, regardless of its functionality. The steganography and cryptography methods could be replaced with any method that proved its resiliency, whether from the state-of-art or customized for this application.

In the next chapter, we explain a lightweight implementation as a proof-of-concept of this designed framework. In the framework, we selected Advanced Encryption Standard (AES) for encryption, LSB for steganography, SHA256 for hashing, and a technological gadget description AR app as the innocuous normal mode part. We studied the security level of this implementation, which was found to be secure even though our selected implementations for the security algorithms were not the strongest among the available.

REFERENCES

1. "Augmented Reality vs. Virtual Reality vs. Mixed Reality: An Introductory Guide," Toptal, 16 January 2026. [Online]. Available: https://www.toptal.com/designers/ui/augmented-reality-vs-virtual-reality-vs-mixed-reality. [Accessed 23 March 2026].
2. Li, Chuanlong; Sun, Xingming; Li, Yuqian, "Information hiding based on Augmented Reality," *Mathematical Biosciences and Engineering*, vol. 16, no. 5, pp. 4777–4787, 2019.
3. Sloane, B., "System for implementing steganography-based augmented reality platform". United States of America Patent US-11551426-B2, 10 January 2023.
4. Wilson, S., *Unreal Steganography: Using A VR Application As A Steganography Carrier*, Sheffield, UK: Sheffield Hallam University, Forensic Focus, 16 July 2019.

Building a Proof-of-Concept

6

6.1 INTRODUCTION

This chapter provides a detailed account of the development process behind our proof-of-concept, which introduces a novel application of steganography within an augmented reality (AR) environment. The primary goal of this work is to seamlessly extend the traditional two-dimensional computer world into the physical realm, allowing digital information to be hidden and retrieved within real-world contexts. To ensure transparency and reproducibility, we structure this chapter to follow the logical flow of the system's architecture, moving from the underlying technical infrastructure to the user-facing elements and, finally, to security validation.

We begin by examining the backend building process, which forms the foundation of the entire system. This section walks through the essential steps required to establish a functional development environment using the Unity engine, a standard platform for creating AR experiences. We describe how the dataset was prepared, including the collection and preprocessing of images necessary for deep learning (DL). Furthermore, we explain the training process of our AI model, detailing how we optimized its performance to balance accuracy with processing speed. This part of the chapter also clarifies the specific encryption and steganography methods employed, explaining how data is secured and concealed before it is ever presented to the user.

Following the backend infrastructure, we depict the frontend building process, which focuses on the user experience. Here, we discuss the design of the interface, emphasizing usability and intuitiveness within an AR context. We explain how the system translates complex backend operations into simple interactions, allowing users to engage with the augmented environment without needing technical expertise. This section highlights the decisions

DOI: 10.1201/9781042003860-7

made to ensure that the hidden data remains invisible to the naked eye while remaining accessible through the application.

Finally, the chapter concludes with a comprehensive security analysis designed to test the resilience of our proof-of-concept. We employ an attack tree methodology, a structured approach that maps out potential security threats and vulnerability paths. By systematically analyzing how an adversary might attempt to breach the system, we can identify weaknesses and demonstrate the strength of our security measures. This analysis not only validates the robustness of the proposed solution but also provides a clear understanding of the security posture maintained throughout the development lifecycle.

6.2 PROOF-OF-CONCEPT BACKEND BUILDING

Our application is composed of a backend part, which we describe in this section, and a front-end part, which we explain in the next section. As we have described in the previous chapter, hiding, also known as embedding, is object-triggered. As such, the first step was to be able to detect the objects. Therefore, the backend of this Stego-AR app used object detection model that we shortened as AI-Part; then our application has to be able to extend the cyber world to the real world. For that, we needed to work on augmenting reality and we call that phase the AR-part. Finally, our application's essential purpose is to hide data, which we further strengthened using encryption; we call that part the Security-part. In Figure 6.1, we remind the reader about the

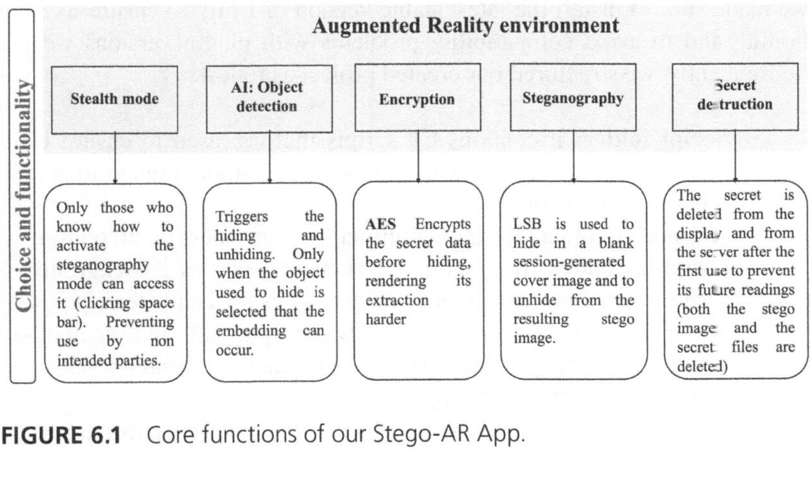

FIGURE 6.1 Core functions of our Stego-AR App.

key five building blocks of our application, their function and how they are implemented in this proof-of-concept version.

Figure 6.2. gives the process of building both roles in the backend and frontend phases. Figure 6.3 illustrates how our proof-of-concept implementation was made to be used. It shows the normal mode denoted as Role 1, which illustrates in an augmented reality environment the technical description of the detected object (mouse) when pointing the phone camera to it from the app environment. Upon activating the second role, which is the steganographic mode, the detected object is selected as trigger; the file is encrypted using the passphrase and is hidden. The unhiding is done by the recipient upon activating Role 2 and using the same trigger object and passphrase.

In what follows, we explain the building process of each part essentially, the AR, AI and security.

6.2.1 AR-Part: Setting Up AR Environment Using Unity

Before we see the development process, it is essential to set up the Unity environment to support backend integration. This includes installing necessary plugins thatwe will be mentioning in the coming sections, setting up project dependencies, and configuring the development environment to handle backend services effectively.

Originally, Unity is a multi-platform game engine created by Unity Technologies. It was initially announced in June 2005 at the Apple Worldwide Developers Conference as a Mac OS X game engine. It supports a wide range of platforms, including desktop, mobile, console and virtual reality environments [1].

Knowing that we will use object detection models from within it later, we made sure to install the latest stable version of Unity to ensure its functioning and to avoid compatibility problems with plugin versions we use. Subsequently, we structured our created project as follows:

- **Script folder:** It contains C# scripts that are used to ensure UI interactivity and functionality, and to ensure smooth integration of AI model into Unity.
- **Animation folder:** It contains animation controllers for all buttons.
- **Graphics folder:** It contains UI elements such as a background sprite (sprites are 2D graphic objects used for characters, props, projectiles and other elements of 2D gameplay [2]) and the application's logo. All of which are used to create the frontend that we demonstrate in the next chapter.
- **SQL folder:** It contains C#-MySQL driver for connection to database.

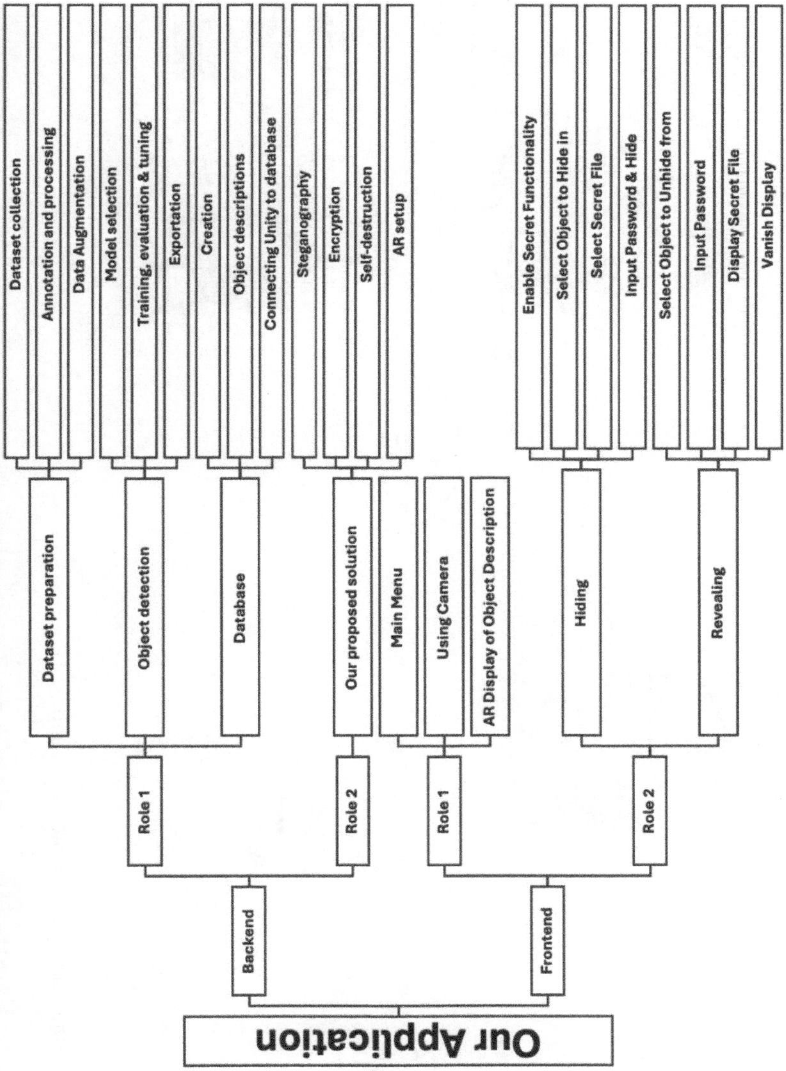

FIGURE 6.2 The process of development of our Stego-AR app.

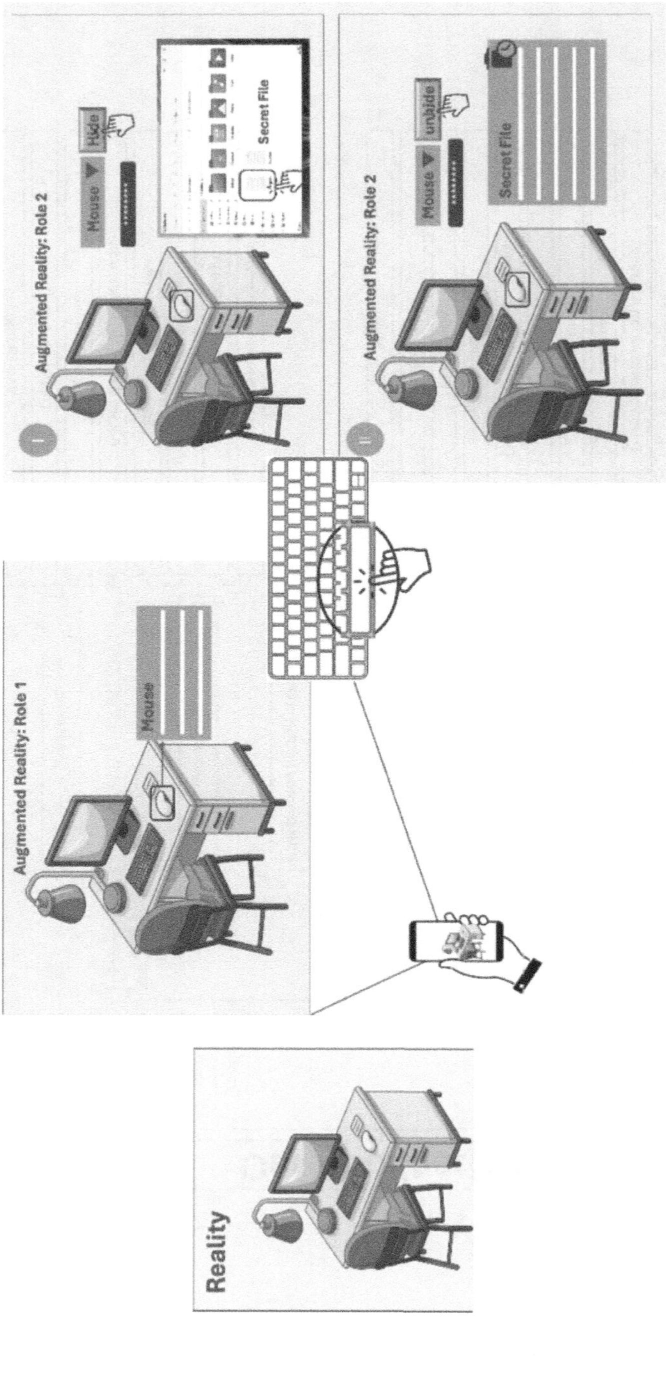

FIGURE 6.3 Functioning of our Stego-AR app.

Following, we install the Sentis plugin, which is a framework for importing and running third-party AI models through the Unity Runtime on user devices [68]; in other words, it is a neural network inference library for Unity. The version used in developing our AR application is 1.3.0 pre-release.

We also setup our database in this phase; the database is currently composed of one table that stores the ten selected objects and their corresponding brief description. It is hosted locally using XAMPP server and interrogated directly from our Stego-AR app using SQL queries from within specified C# script. It will be expanded in the future with user accounts and subscriptions.

6.2.2 AI-Part: Object Detection

In this part, we explain the model we selected for the object detection part, the dataset collection and preparation phase, followed by the model training phase, then the last phase related to saving it, importing it and using it from Unity.

6.2.2.1 Dataset preparation

The innocuous part of the application – generic role – is focused on its ability to recognize a list of objects and display their description overlaid on the real scene. That is what a normal user will be using the app for. Initially, while we tested the Unity setup, we used the Yolov8s pretrained model, which was trained on COCO dataset. At this phase, we wanted to confirm that object detection can occur successfully from within Unity. In matter of fact, we intended to keep using that model, because its mAP50-95 was acceptable of 44.9 [3] and it recognizes 80 objects. However, upon further observations of the objects it detects, which were mainly animals, fruits, vegetables, transportation means, etc., we had to think of retraining YOLOv8s on a dataset of our selection. The dataset contained random objects that did not match the scope of the prototype we are making. We wanted an application that describes digital-/office-related devices/tools – first because it relates to our field of study, second because they are widely available. These were our motivations; they were made for the sake of this prototype. However, it is important to highlight that in real deployment of the application, the more objects it recognizes the better, the more varied the merrier as it would mean having larger client base. We recapped the object names of COCO dataset by category in Table 6.1.

As mentioned earlier, in this prototype, we decided to select ten digital devices, which are computer mouse, keyboard, smartwatch, laptop, wireless earbuds, phone charger, smart phone, video projector, hard disk and USB

TABLE 6.1 COCO 2017 dataset objects per category

CATEGORY	*OBJECTS*
Transportation	Bicycle, car, motorcycle, airplane, bus, train, truck, boat, traffic light, fire hydrant, stop sign, parking meter
Animals	Bench, bird, cat, dog, horse, sheep, cow, elephant, bear, zebra, giraffe
Accessories	Backpack, umbrella, handbag, tie, suitcase
Sports	Frisbee, skis, snowboard, sports ball, kite, baseball bat, baseball glove, skateboard, surfboard, tennis racket
Food	Bottle, wine glass, cup, fork, knife, spoon, bowl, banana, apple, sandwich, orange, broccoli, carrot, hot dog, pizza, donut, cake
Furniture	Chair, couch, potted plant, bed. dining table, toilet, sink, refrigerator
Household items	Book, clock, vase, scissors, teddy bear, toothbrush
Electronics	TV, laptop, mouse, remote, keyboard, cell phone, microwave, oven, toaster, hair dryer

flash drive. The images of our dataset were self-collected from the internet, we resume the number of images per each object for training, testing and validating in Table 6.2.

The next step was to label the data and specify the objects' locations (surround it with a box), and also to add their annotation or identity. For this purpose, we used Roboflow, a framework to label, train and deploy computer vision solutions [4], to annotate the images. Furthermore, since the original dataset had a total of 2992 images with an average of 299 pictures per class, we assumed from previous experiences that it was not enough to get accurate detection results; so we decided to apply data augmentation techniques that provide us with the ability to generate additional pictures from our original dataset to extend it. These images are generated by applying random and realistic transform operations such as image rotation, saturation, zooming, etc. on our original images [5]. The training dataset was extended to 5654 images. Roboflow [6] was also used for this phase, and it automatically labeled the generated data based on the original dataset. Moreover, we used it to unify the size of pictures to 640×640. It offers multiple options to export the dataset; we used the option that allows us to use it directly from Google Drive. We resume in Table 6.3 the dataset size per class after the data augmentation for the training, validation and testing splits.

TABLE 6.2 Number of images of our collected dataset per object per split

OBJECTS	*COMPUTER MOUSE*	*KEYBOARD*	*SMART WATCH*	*LAPTOP*	*WIRELESS EARBUDS*	*PHONE CHARGER*	*SMART PHONE*	*VIDEO PROJECTOR*	*HARD DISK*	*USB FLASH DRIVE*
Train	100	304	113	193	369	190	162	199	366	109
Valid	30	84	21	60	113	40	72	47	107	31
Test	14	51	18	20	53	8	32	15	60	11

TABLE 6.3 Number of images of our collected dataset per object per split after Augmentation

OBJECTS	*COMPUTER MOUSE*	*KEYBOARD*	*SMART WATCH*	*LAPTOP*	*WIRELESS EARBUDS*	*PHONE CHARGER*	*SMART PHONE*	*VIDEO PROJECTOR*	*HARD DISK*	*USB FLASH DRIVE*
Train	290	869	237	520	968	324	434	555	1052	405
Valid	30	84	21	60	113	40	72	47	107	31
Test	14	51	18	20	53	8	32	15	60	11

6.2.2.2 Training YOLOv8s

For the training, we seeded the dataset composed of ten classes and 6.5K images and trained using YOLOv8s pretrained model for 350 epochs with one ".yaml" file that contains classes and path to its data. To use Google Colab for the training, we had to setup few things first, we need to connect it with our Google Drive. Then, we installed YOLOv8 dependencies in our project folder and proceeded to the training.

- Training Results

As we mentioned in Section 6.2.2.2, the training was done using the YOLOv8s pretrained model. Because of Google Colab resource allocation restrictions, the training session was not done continuously on one-go and was divided on multiple rounds. Each round's duration depended on the remaining available time for using the resources, leading to training sessions of varying lengths: 15 epochs, 40 epochs and sometimes 70 epochs. Each new round used the weight "best.pt" of the previous round as input, this was possible thanks to the *transfer training* technique, which was allowed by YOLOv8. Once the training is finished, the results are saved in runs/train folder. The results of the last round are shown in Figures 6.5–6.8.

The evaluation metrics calculated during the training and validation phases by YOLOv8 are resumed and saved at the end of each training. The metrics include:

- **Recall** is the ratio between the number of positive samples correctly classified as positive to the total number of positive samples. It measures the model's ability to detect actual positive samples. The higher the recall, the more positive samples detected [7].

$$Recall = \frac{True_{positive}}{True_{positive} + False_{negative}} \tag{6.1}$$

- **Precision** is calculated as the ratio between the number of positive samples correctly classified to the total number of samples classified as positive (either correctly or incorrectly). The precision measures the model's accuracy in classifying a sample as positive [7].

$$Precision = \frac{True_{positive}}{True_{positive} + False_{positve}} \tag{6.2}$$

- **Confusion Matrix** is a tool that evaluates the performance of a classification model by tabulating true positive, true negative, false positive and false negative predictions. It compares the actual target values with those predicted by the machine learning model [8].

- **Mean Average Precision** (mAP) is the mean of the average precision scores for each class in the dataset. It gives a single number that summarizes the performance of the model across all classes. Referring to Figure 6.4, we can notice that mAP is calculated with the use of these four metrics (confusion matrix, precision, recall and intersection over union) [9].

From these metrics, we can evaluate the performance of our model. In our case, we obtained good accuracy from the metrics. The results of the last round of 40 epochs of the training are shown in Figures 6.5–6.8.

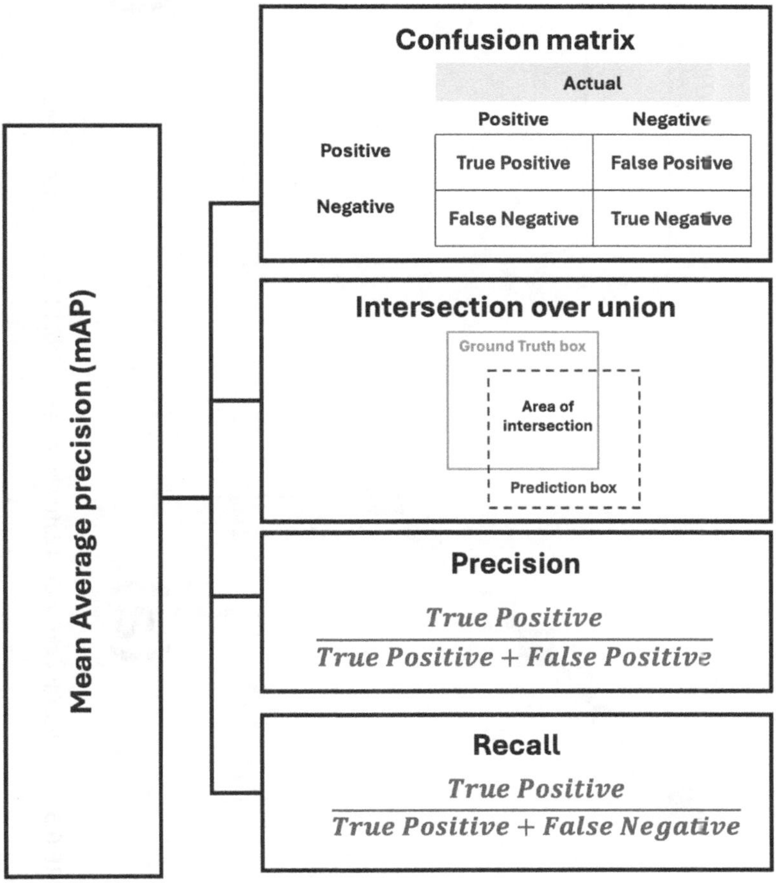

FIGURE 6.4 Mean Average Precision (mAP).

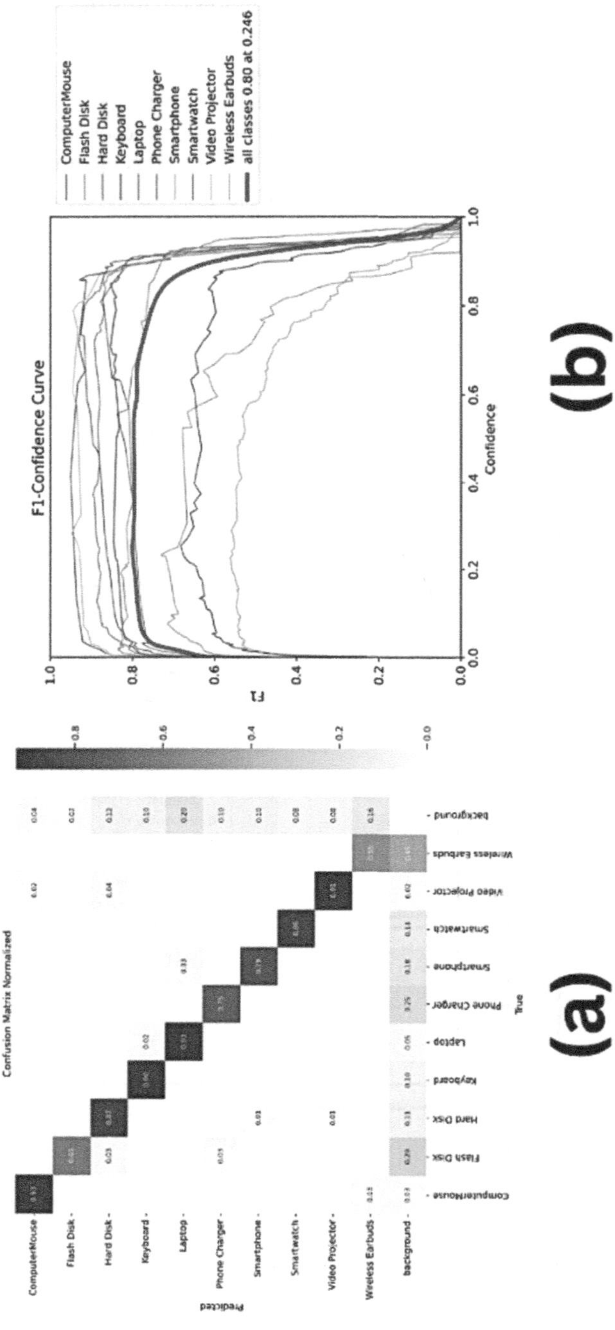

FIGURE 6.5 Results: (a) Confusion Matrix Normalized, (b) F1-Confidence Curve.

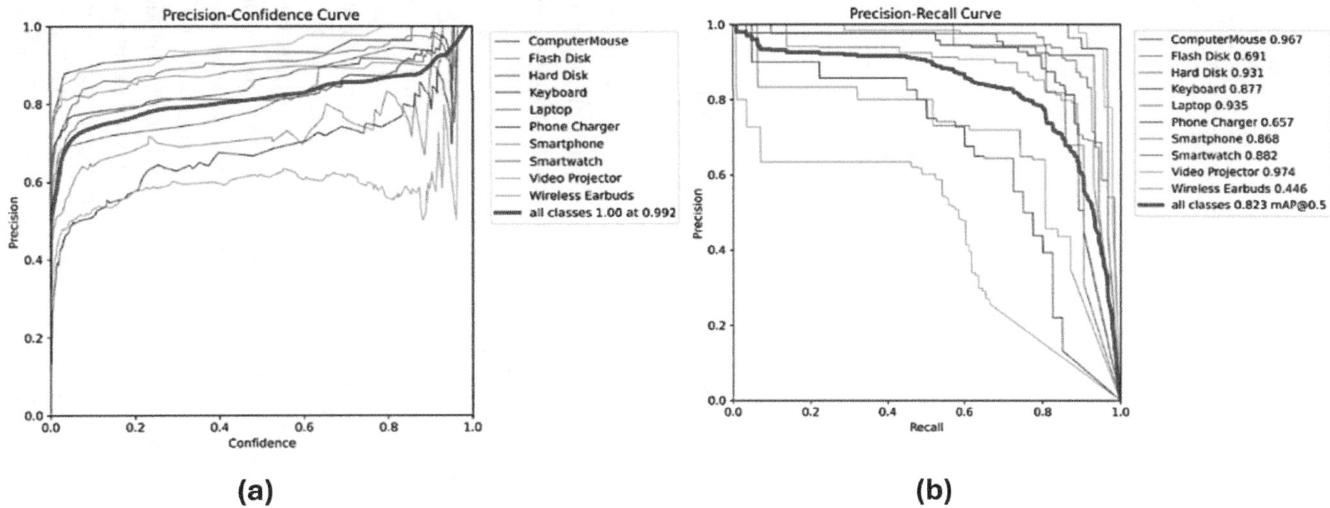

FIGURE 6.6 Results: (a) Precision-Confidence Curve, (b) Precision-Recall Curve.

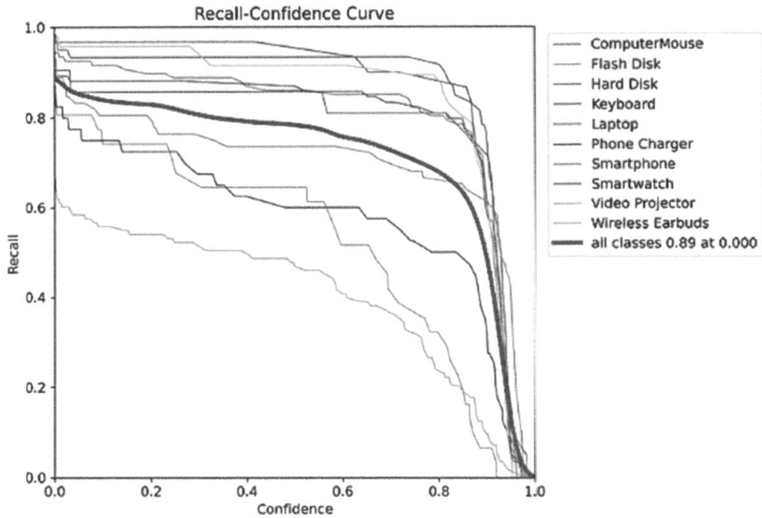

FIGURE 6.7 Recall-Confidence Curve.

The normalized confusion matrix scales the values in the confusion matrix to reflect proportions instead of raw counts. This makes it easier to compare performance across classes. Referring to Figure 6.5 (a), we can see that the diagonal has high values. These values represent the proportion of correct predictions for each class. Higher values indicate better performance for that class. The rest of the matrix is almost clean, with low values indicating few misclassification cases.

The *F1 score* is the mean of precision and recall, providing a single metric to evaluate the balance between precision and recall. The peak of the F1-confidence curve indicates the confidence threshold that provides the best balance between precision and recall. This is often the threshold we might want to use for classifying detections as positive, which is in our case **0.80** (refer to Figure 6.5 (b)). An increased confidence threshold leads to higher precision but lower recall. This means fewer false positives but more false negatives. A decreased confidence threshold leads to higher recall but lower precision. This means fewer false positives but more false negatives.

A high precision is noticed at high confidence thresholds in Figure 6.6 (a) indicating that the model is very accurate when it is most confident about its predictions. This means that false positives are rare when the model is certain.

The curve closer to the top-right corner in Figure 6.6 (b) indicates better performance, with high precision and high recall at **0.82**. A high recall is maintained across a wide range of thresholds in Figure 6.7 indicating a strong model. As shown in Figure 6.8, the mAP of all classes is **0.8.**

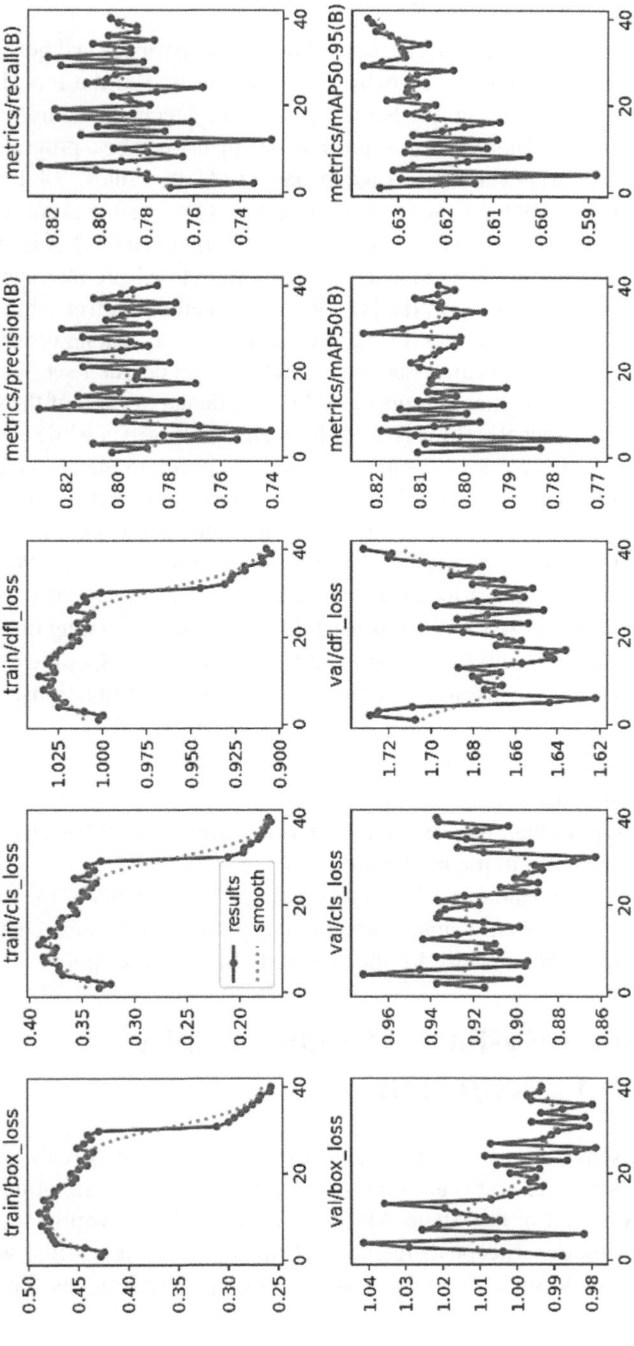

FIGURE 6.8 Summarized results of the last 40 epochs.

6.2.2.3 Using the model in Unity

After we were able to conduct a successful training experience and got satisfied with the model's good accuracy (which is 80%), we passed the model to our Unity application. Knowing that Sentis framework, which is a neural network inference library for Unity. It was a "pre-release" in an open beta program available to all Unity users via the package manager in Unity Editor [10]. It accepts Open Neural Network Exchange (ONNX) format; we needed to export our custom saved model in Colab to this ONNX format. Noting that ONNX is an open-source format that aims to provide a common format to ensure interoperability between different DL frameworks [11]. We encountered an error while trying to import the ONNX model into Unity indicating that, after long research, the Sentis framework accepts an opset version (refers to an operator set, which is a collection of operators that are supported by a particular version of the ONNX specification) between 9 and 15. That is why we had to specify it while exporting.

To integrate the model in Unity, we need to import it in the assets folder in our project, then we had to serialize it to "StreamingAssets" using the inspector window (it opens by clicking on the model) and then click on the button "Serialize to StreamingAssets" to obtain a file in ".sentis" format. We had to do the previous step for various reasons such as, firstly, it is validated in Unity, secondly, to save disk space in our project, finally, for faster loading times [12].

To work with the model, we load it in Unity. We made a specific C# script file for the real-time inference that manages the following functions:

- Opening the webcam.
- Loading the model.
- Setting up the input by capturing video frames at 30 fps and then feeding them to the model for inference.
- Saving the results in a list that composes the elements of the drop-down component whose role will be explained in the next chapter.
- Fetching the database for the detected object's description.

6.2.3 Security-Part: Steganography and Encryption

We have discussed earlier the backend from the augmented reality aspect, which represents the first role of AR app; in this section, we are going to see the security aspect of our Stego-AR app. The second role ensures the secret file remains hidden except to intended recipient. To achieve this, we have opted to combine steganography with cryptography techniques for adding extra layer of security.

For steganography, we have chosen the LSB algorithm for several reasons including its simplicity, ease of implementation and its ability to effectively embed secret files within stego-images. The algorithm was implemented in C# making it compatible with our Unity project. Currently, the app accepts only ".txt" files as secret files. Thanks to *FileNativePicker* package, we were able to provide users with the ability to pick the secret file from their internal storage. Once selected, the file is parsed and then embedded into the cover image according to the object selected from the list of detected objects by our custom-trained AI model. Unhiding the secret follows a similar approach but in reverse; the user selects the appropriate object – the same object by his/her camera as the one used in the embedding – then, clicks the unhide button. If the object is different than the one selected during the hiding process, the revealing process is not successful; if the object is the same, the revealing process is successful and the secret file is displayed to the intended user. Once finished, the display is cleared, and the file is destroyed, leaving no traces of the exchanged secret.

To enforce the security, we combined steganography with encryption; the secret file is first encrypted then hidden. When the intended party attempts to reveal the secret, it must know the object triggering the embedding process and the password used to create the encryption key; the secret file is first restored, then decrypted, before it is displayed. At last, once read, it is destroyed and vanishes from the display. For encryption purposes, we used the Advanced Encryption Standard (AES) algorithm with a key of 128 bits and implemented it in C# because it is a symmetric encryption algorithm known for its security and efficiency.

In our application, when selecting the secret file, the user is prompted to enter a password of 16 characters. The latter is used to encrypt the stego-file. The same password is required for decryption to complete. For further security enhancement, the password used in encryption and decryption is stored hashed. For the password hashing, we used SHA256.

We remind the reader that this is a prototype implementation for proof-of-concept aims. Both steganography and cryptography methods chosen here shall be replaced by stronger ones in the real-world elaboration phase.

6.3 PROOF-OF-CONCEPT FRONTEND BUILDING

Before we explain the creation process of the frontend, let us first explore the views of our Stego-AR application. The application comprises two scenes, referred to as "main menu" and "AppScene" within Unity. The "main menu"

FIGURE 6.9 The Main Menu scene.

scene serves as a welcoming interface for users to guide them on how the app is used and showcases its functionalities using AR technology developed with the use of the Vuforia SDK. The second scene is the core of the application; it includes both roles: Role 1 for AR object description (generic mode) and Role 2 for steganography in which we employed object detection, AR, steganography and encryption techniques (steganographic mode). Figure 6.9 illustrates the "main menu" scene, both with and without AR, while Figure 6.10 represents the "AppScene".

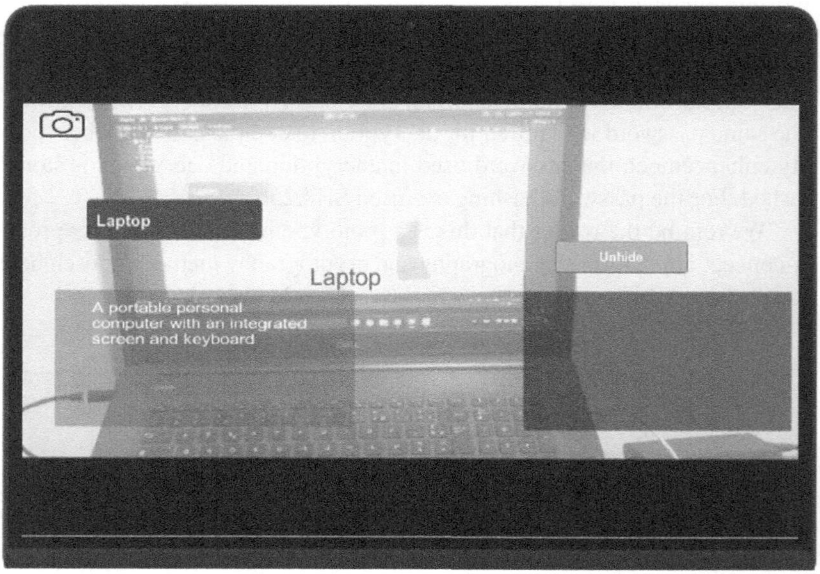

FIGURE 6.10 The AppScene view.

To create the main menu scene, we used Vuforia from Unity. To set up Vuforia with Unity, we first downloaded the Vuforia SDK. After that, we imported it into our Unity project. Next, we generated a License key from the Vuforia Developer Portal website and added it to our Vuforia Configuration file. Upon doing so, Vuforia elements would be present in Unity.

Then, we had to set up the image target from which we extend the application to the real world to add the augmented reality functionalities. To do so, we prepared the image in a particular way; first we created as our target image a QR code of our application's name. In the real-world elaboration version, this QR code could be generated from the link of the user's space in our hosted AR app server. Subsequently, we uploaded the QR code image to Vuforia database, then processed it to get its augmentation score. Note that only if the augmentation score exceeds three stars out of five, a picture can be used as an image target. Our QR code image received a five-stars rating (refer to Figure 6.11). It is worth mentioning that Image Targets in Unity have certain restrictions. These include:

- Image Targets can be created using JPG or PNG images in RGB or greyscale format.
- The size of the input images must be 2.25 MB or less.
- The images must have a minimum width of 320 pixels.

FIGURE 6.11 The augmentation score and features of the target in Vuforia database.

Then, from Unity project, within the inspector of the ImageTarget GameObject, we selected the imported database that we have downloaded from our workspace on Vuforia Developer Website. This database contains our target image, and then choose the QR code target. Once finished, we can create any GameObject as a child of this *ImageTarget*, and it gets displayed when detecting the target in real-world scene.

Now that we have created the augmented environment, we can add its elements. As seen in Figure 6.9 (left part), our augmented environment contains a virtual start button, a video explaining the functioning of our application, an avatar and information about the developer and his picture (the second author of this book).

To create a virtual button, we navigate to the Image Target Behaviour tab within the Image Target. Under the Advanced Options, we select "Add Virtual Button". This action generates a blue-colored virtual button within the game scene. We adjust the button's position and size to suit the target image. In the Inspector panel, under Virtual Button Behaviour, we can fine-tune sensitivity settings as required (we set it to "High" for a better experience). This option facilitates tailored interactions for our augmented reality application. We attach a C# script to the virtual button, ensuring its functionality of loading the "AppScene" once a hand passes into the virtual area. The script contains the necessary logic to trigger the transition to the "AppScene" upon detecting hand movement within the specified region. See the start button in Figure 6.9 for the illustration of the virtual button overlaied virtually on top of the real QR Code label; the button is seen from the phone and is clicked upon hovering over its position in real world (on air over the QR Code) by hand.

To incorporate the illustrative video, we create a Plane game object as a child of ImageTarget. We then attach a video player component to it. Next, we import the video in our assets folder. Finally, we drag and drop the video file into the video player component attached to the Plane GameObject. To ensure that the video sound plays only when the object is detected and not when the app runs, we uncheck the option "Play on Awake" for the video component. We choose to put an illustrative video instead of a textual guide for two reasons. The first reason is that videos are more effective in conveying app functionality compared to readme files or other forms of documentation. The second reason is that we aimed to show the power of AR technology and inject an element of fun into the video to engage users and prevent monotony. The video is created using an online animation video creator "Animaker" [13]. This tool provides you with the ability to create your own cartoon character with multiple gestures, to add text and elements and to export the video.

For the avatar standing and rotating intermittently, we custom-created it to look like the first author. We used for that an online avatar creator for

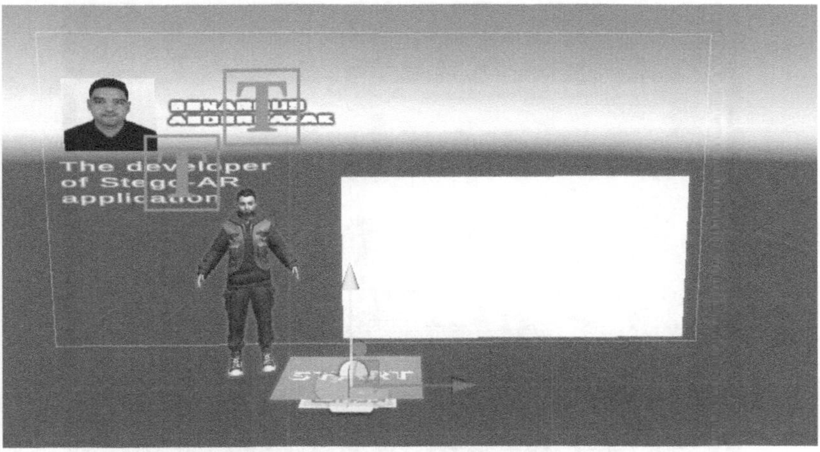

FIGURE 6.12 The final design of "Main Scene" in Unity Editor with virtual button.

games called "Ready Player Me" [14]. Then, we downloaded Ready Player Me SDK for Unity and imported it into our project. After that, we generated an API key on the Ready Player Me website and copied this API key into the avatar loader in Unity. Later, we create a script to make the avatar rotate at regular intervals. The final design of our main scene from within Unity is illustrated in Figure 6.12.

6.3.1 Role 01: Generic Mode – AR Object Description

Role 01 focuses on real-time object detection using the custom-trained AI model. We already explained the training part in the backend; now we explore the frontend that uses it mainly in "AppScene" view. The user points the camera towards an object, if the model recognizes the object, then its description is fetched from the database and displayed in the left part of the screen (refer to Figure 6.13).

6.3.2 Role 02: Steganographic Mode

In Role 02 depicted in Figure 6.14, which focuses on security, we delve into the frontend design of the "AppScene" and its integration with the backend

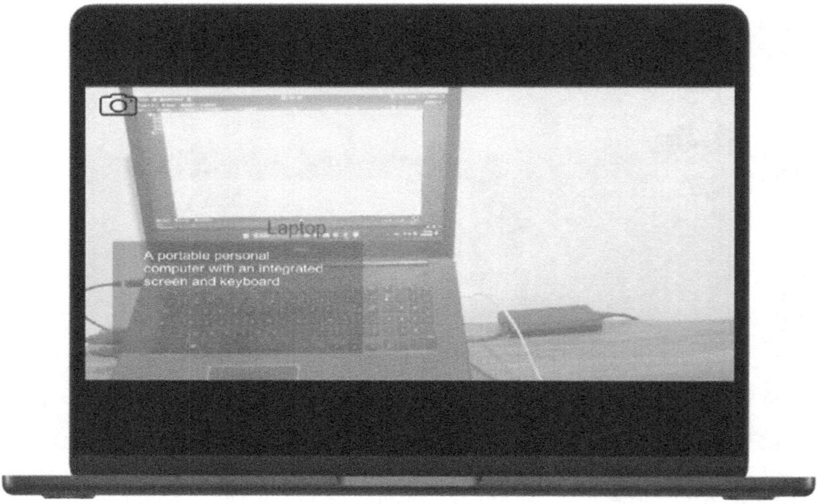

FIGURE 6.13 Role 01: Detecting object and displaying its description.

logic discussed earlier. To enter this mode, the user holds the space button on the keyboard to enable the secret functionality. By doing so, instead of displaying the objects description only, a drop-down list containing all the detected objects from the captured scene is displayed to the user. The objects are detected in real time from the camera-captured scene. Upon

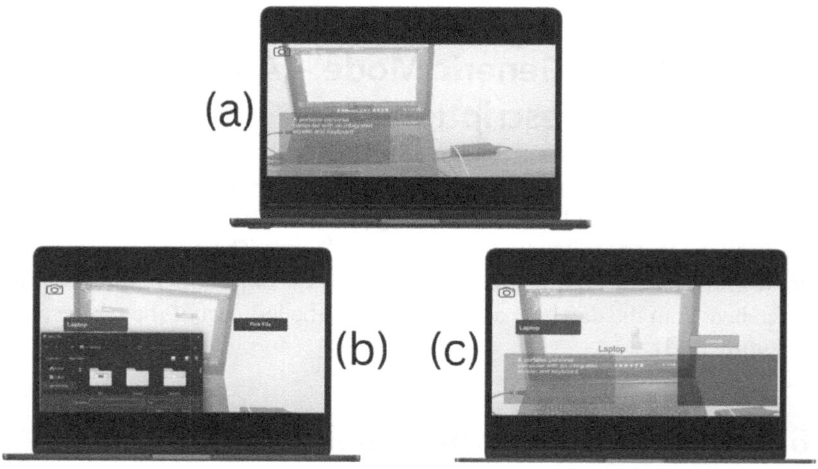

FIGURE 6.14 (a) Detected objects added to Drop Down component, (b) Picking the secret file, (c) Unhide process.

selecting an object to trigger the hiding, two new buttons are displayed to the user; the first is "pick file", and the second is "hide". The "Pick File" allows the user to pick the secret file from his/her internal storage. To enhance the design of the button, we decided to incorporate an animation effect. When the user hovers over the button, it scales up to a larger size, and when the user moves the cursor away, the button returns to its initial size. Upon selecting the file, a password field appears to the user to encrypt the secret file with an indication that the password should be composed of 16 characters. Upon clicking the "Hide/Submit" button, the encrypted secret file is hidden.

To reveal the secret file, first the user has to enter the second role (steganography mode) and then has to select the same object used to hide the secret. We mean well the object by its type not necessarily the exact same picture of the object. Upon doing so, the "Unhide" button is displayed; this button also incorporates the same design concept and animation as the previous ones. When the unhide button is clicked, the user is asked to provide the password to decrypt the file, the same password used to encrypt the file because as we have explained in the previous chapter, we are using AES symmetric key encryption method. After which, the secret message is displayed in clear text in a display area. Each line of the file is displayed using a typing animation effect sequentially. Only one line is visible at a time, and there is no option to revisit the content once displayed, as it vanishes afterward, because the secret file is destroyed once read, as explained in the backend section.

To recap, the user unaware of the functioning principle would think that the hiding is done in the selected object, and the beautiful part is that the unhiding can be done using the same object type without necessarily having it. Let us explain, for example, the use scenario from the point of view of users. Assuming that we have two users, say A and B; they want to exchange a secret file without raising suspicions. Let A be the first author and B be the second author and the secret file being this book while in the drafting phase. Authors A and B agree on a common passphrase, the use of our application, and the object being the computer mouse. The method both authors A and B agreed on for setting these is out of the scope of this research and is assumed to be secure; it can be face to face, via phone, encrypted email, etc. When user A wants to send the file to user B, A will first run the AR app and then enter the steganographic mode by enabling the secret functionality through clicking and holding the space bar. Then, A detects the computer mouse using the camera, selects the secret file, type the password and the file gets hidden as intended. User B uses the same app, detects a computer mouse, that could be of different brand, shape and color, enters the passphrase and reads in the AR display the secret file before it vanishes.

6.4 ANALYSIS

We have shown that the proposed system is designed as a secure steganography framework that combines AI, AR and encryption to exchange secret files in an innocent and non-suspicious manner. In the presented proof-of-concept, the AES and LSB algorithms were selected for encryption and steganography, respectively, because they are easy to implement, rather than because they provide the highest level of security. Since the system operates correctly with these techniques, it can be further strengthened by replacing them with more advanced and secure encryption and steganography methods. In this section, we focus on analyzing the security of the proposed scheme. To assess its security, we employ an attack tree model to formally describe how an adversary might achieve the main objective, which is gaining access to the secret file. Attack trees break down a high-level attack goal into smaller sub-goals and basic actions, and they represent the logical relationships between these steps using "AND" and "OR" nodes. The resulting attack tree is illustrated in Figure 6.15. To further support the analysis, the attack tree is combined with probability theory in order to estimate the likelihood that an attacker can successfully achieve the main attack goal.

Assuming that:

- p_s = the probability to successfully steal stego file
- p_b = the probability that the attacker can break the steganography method used

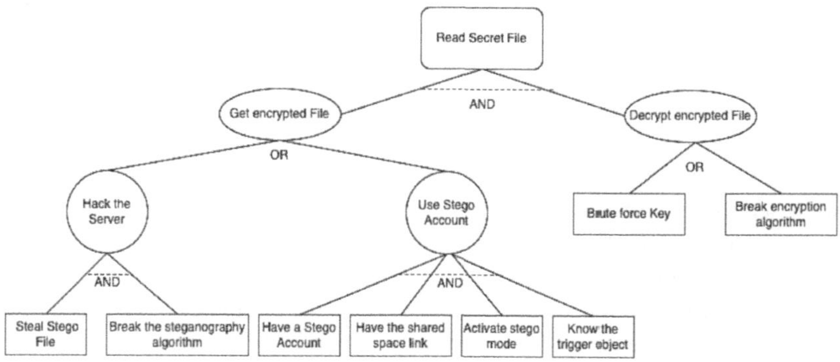

FIGURE 6.15 Attack Tree for breaking our AR-based steganography method to read the secret file.

- p_a = the probability to have stego account
- p_l = the probability to know shared space link
- p_m = the probability that the attacker knows how to activate stego mode
- p_t = the probability that the attacker knows the trigger object
- p_f = the probability to successfully Brute-force key within a deterministic time
- p_c = the probability to know and break encryption algorithm

To compute the probability of achieving the subgoals $[15]$, we start from the bottom up to the root. The "AND" node is translated as a multiplication, and the "OR" node is translated as: 1- $\prod_{i=1}^{n}(1-P_i)$.

In the attack tree, two main subgoals are defined: "Get encrypted file" and "Decrypt encrypted file". To calculate the probability of achieving the first subgoal, denoted as P(Get encrypted file), two alternative attack paths are considered: "Hack the server" or "Use Stego Account". Therefore, the probability of achieving this subgoal is computed as P(Hack the server) OR P(Use Stego Account). The probability of "Hack the server" is calculated in Equation (6.3) by applying an AND relationship between its leaf nodes. In a similar manner, the probability of "Use Stego Account" is computed in Equation (6.4).

$$P(Hack\,the\,server) = p_s \cdot p_b \tag{6.3}$$

$$P(Use\,Stego\,Account) = p_a \cdot p_l \cdot p_m \cdot p_t \tag{6.4}$$

From Equations (6.3) and (6.4), we compute the probability of getting the encrypted file successfully P(Get encrypted file) by applying the (6.3) OR (6.4), the calculations are given in Equations (6.5) and (6.6)

$$\begin{aligned} &P(Get\,encrypted\,file) \\ &= 1 - (1 - P(Hack\,the\,server))(1 - P(Use\,Stego\,Account)) \end{aligned} \tag{6.5}$$

$$P(Get\,encrypted\,file) = 1 - (1 - (p_s \cdot p_b))(1 - (p_a \cdot p_l \cdot p_m \cdot p_t)) \tag{6.6}$$

To compute the probability to decrypt the encrypted file P(**Decrypt encrypted file**), we apply OR to its leaves, the calculation is illustrated in Equation (6.7):

$$P(Decrypt\,encrypted\,file) = 1 - (1 - p_f)(1 - p_c) \tag{6.7}$$

The probability to achieve the final aim, which is that an adversary can successfully read the secret file, is computed using Equations (6.6) and (6.7) as demonstrated in Equations (6.8) and (6.9).

$$P(\textit{Read secret file}) = P(\textit{Get encrypted file}) \times P(\textit{Decrypt encrypted file}) \tag{6.8}$$

$$P(\textit{Read secret file}) = \left[1-\left(1-(p_s \cdot p_b)\right)\times\left(1-(p_a \cdot p_l \cdot p_m \cdot p_t)\right)\right] \times\left[1-(1-p_f)(1-p_c)\right] \tag{6.9}$$

Since we want to analyze the security of our designed system, we consider first the following scenarios:

- **Scenario 1:** The attacker would certainly read the secret file $\left(P(\textit{Read secret file})=1\right)$
- **Scenario 2:** The attacker would never be able to read the secret file $\left(P(\textit{Read secret file})=0\right)$

We consider that Equation (6.9) is simplified to: $P = A \times B$

$$A = 1-(1-p_s p_b)(1-p_a p_l p_m p_t)$$

$$B = 1-(1-p_f)(1-p_c)$$

- In Scenario 1: P=A × B=1 ⇒ A=1 AND B=1

$$\mathbf{A=1} \Rightarrow 1-(1-p_s p_b)(1-p_a p_l p_m p_t)=1$$

Thus, $(1-p_s p_b)(1-p_a p_l p_m p_t)=0 \Rightarrow (1-p_s p_b)=0$ **OR** $(1-p_a p_l p_m p_t)=0$

Hence, $p_s p_b = 1 \Rightarrow p_s = p_b = 1$

OR

$$p_a p_l p_m p_t = 1 \Rightarrow p_a = p_l = p_m = p_t = 1$$

$$\mathbf{B=1} \Rightarrow 1-(1-p_f)(1-p_c)=1$$

$$\Rightarrow (1-p_f)(1-p_c)=0 \Rightarrow (1-p_f)=0 \textbf{ OR } (1-p_c)=0$$

Hereford, $p_f = 1$ **OR** p_c=1.

Henceforth, for **Scenario 1** to be achieved, Attacker is guaranteed to get the stego file AND Attacker is guaranteed to break its protection.

- **In Scenario 2: P=A×B=0 ⇒ A=0 OR B=0**

$$\mathbf{A = 0} \Rightarrow 1-(1-p_s p_b)(1-p_a p_l p_m p_t) = 0 \Rightarrow (1-p_s p_b)(1-p_a p_l p_m p_t) = 1$$

$$\Rightarrow (1-p_s p_b) = 1 \ \textbf{AND} \ (1-p_a p_l p_m p_t) = 1$$

$$(1-p_s p_b) = 1 \Rightarrow p_s p_b = 0 \Rightarrow p_s = 0 \ \textbf{OR} \ p_b = 0$$

$$(1-p_a p_l p_m p_t) = 1 \Rightarrow p_a p_l p_m p_t = 0 \Rightarrow p_a = 0 \ \textbf{OR} \ p_l = 0 \ \textbf{OR} \ p_m = 0 \ \textbf{OR} \ p_t = 0$$

$$\mathbf{B = 0} \Rightarrow 1-(1-p_f)(1-p_c) = 0 \Rightarrow (1-p_f)(1-p_c) = 1 \Rightarrow (1-p_f) = 1 \textbf{AND} (1-p_c) = 1$$

$$(1-p_f) = 1 \Rightarrow p_f = 0$$

$$(1-p_c) = 1 \Rightarrow p_c = 0$$

Accordingly, for the system to be considered secure, at least one of the following conditions must hold: either an attacker is unable to gain access to the stego content or the attacker is unable to break the protection applied to it. In other words, security can be ensured by preventing access to the hidden data or by employing steganography and encryption methods that are sufficiently strong to resist attacks.

To evaluate the proposed proof-of-concept and to clearly demonstrate the practical use of the attack tree model, we adopt, for illustrative purposes, the probability grid presented in Table 6.4. This grid is used to assign probabilities to the leaf nodes shown in Table 6.5, which are then used to calculate the overall probability of successfully reading the encrypted file in our proof-of-concept system.

We compute the security of our proof-of-concept by replacing the values of the probabilities in Equation (6.9).

$$P(Read\,secret\,file) = \left[\left(1-(1-p_s \cdot p_b)\right) \times \left(1-(p_a \cdot p_l \cdot p_m \cdot p_t)\right)\right] \times \left[1-(1-p_f)(1-p_c)\right]$$

TABLE 6.4 Difficulty grid

DIFFICULTY LEVEL	*ASSUMED PROBABILITY OF SUCCESS*
1 (very easy)	1
2 (easy)	0.75
3 (moderate)	0.5
4 (difficult)	0.25
5 (easy)	0.1

TABLE 6.5 Leaves assumed probability

LEAVE PROBABILITIES	*LEVEL OF DIFFICULTY (5-1)*	*ASSUMED PROBABILITY*
p_s	3	0.5
p_b	2	0.75
p_a	2	0.75
p_l	2	0.75
p_m	1/84 (we suppose that we have 84 key on our keyboard)	0.01
p_t	1/10 (we have ten objects in our study)	0.1
p_f	~0	0
p_c	~0	0

$$P(Read\ secret\ file) = \left[1-\left(1-(0.5*0.75)\right)\times\left(1-(0.75*0.75*0.01*0.1)\right)\right] \times\left[1-(1-0)(1-0)\right]$$

$$P(Read\ secret\ file) = \left[1-(1-0.375)\times(1-0.00056)\right]\times\left[1-(1-0)(1-0)\right]$$

$$P(Read\ secret\ file) = \left[1-(0.625*0.99)\right]\times\mathbf{0} = \mathbf{0.37}\times\mathbf{0} = \mathbf{0}$$

Although our assumed probabilities did not come from empirical experience, the chances of achieving the final goal remains impossible, given the well-known fact that AES and its keys are virtually impossible to break within a realistic timeframe.

6.5 CONCLUSION

In this chapter, we depicted the frontend of our application, including its roles and its relationship with the backend part. This proof-of-concept used AI object detection to detect the objects and show their descriptions in Role 01 and to use them as a hiding trigger in Role 02. We used LSB for the steganography, AES for cryptography and SHA256 for hashing. The AR mobile application is built using Unity, which is a game engine. We selected a text file to embed that is displayed in the AR app and wiped from the display as soon as read and wiped entirely from the app as well. Although we know that our steganography method used is weak, we used it for its ease of implementation. Yet even though we did not use the most resilient choices for security, the attack tree analysis showed that this proof-of-concept is still considered secure. Therefore, we expect the framework to provide a higher security level when using other stronger algorithms.

REFERENCES

1. "Unity (game engine)," Wikipedia, 1 February 2022. [Online]. Available: https://en.wikipedia.org/wiki/Unity_(game_engine). [Accessed 19 April 2024].
2. Unity, "Sprite," Unity. [Online]. Available: https://docs.unity3d.com/ScriptReference/Sprite.html#:~:text=Sprites%20are%202D%20graphic%20objects,used%20for%20a%20specific%20Sprite. [Accessed 21 April 2024].
3. Ultralytics, "COCO Pretrained Models," Ultralytics. [Online]. Available: https://docs.ultralytics.com/datasets/detect/coco/#coco-pretrained-models. [Accessed 28 May 2024].
4. Roboflow, "AI that Sees and Understands the Physical World," Roboflow. [Online]. Available: https://roboflow.com/. [Accessed 23 April 2024].
5. Haba, Duc, *Data Augmentation with Python*, Packt Publishing, 2023.
6. Unity, "sentis," [Online]. Available: https://unity.com/products/sentis. [Accessed 21 April 2024.]
7. Abderrazak, Benarous, *Talk2me: A Real-Time Sign Language Translator*, Laghouat, Algeria: University of Laghouat, 2022.
8. "Confusion Matrix," Encord. [Online]. Available: https://encord.com/glossary/confusion-matrix/. [Accessed 25 May 2024].
9. Ahmed, Nisha, Arya, "Mean Average Precision (mAP): A Complete Guide," Kili Technology, 06 July 2023. [Online]. Available: https://kili-technology.com/data-labeling/machine-learning/mean-average-precision-map-a-complete-guide. [Accessed 24 May 2024].

10. "Sentis Overview," Unity. [Online]. Available: https://docs.unity3d.com/Packages/com.unity.sentis@1.4/manual/index.html. [Accessed 4 May 2024].
11. "Open Neural Network Exchange," ONNX, 2019. [Online]. Available: https://onnx.ai/get-started.html. [Accessed 24 April 2024].
12. "Serialize a Model," Unity. [Online]. Available: https://docs.unity3d.com/Packages/com.unity.sentis@1.3/manual/serialize-a-model.html. [Accessed 24 April 2024].
13. "The Future of Animated Video Making Is Here," Animaker. [Online]. Available: https://www.animaker.com/. [Accessed 10 May 2024].
14. "Ready Player Me," Ready Player Me. [Online]. Available: https://readyplayer.me/. [Accessed 10 May 2024].
15. Bryant, William D., "Predicting cyber attack probability using probabilistic attack trees," *International Test & Evaluation Association (ITEA)*, vol. 46, no. 4. doi: 10.61278/itea.46.4.1002, 2025.

General Conclusion

This book presents the design and development of an application that combines two main functions. On one hand, the system acts as an augmented reality (AR)-based informational tool that helps users learn about electronic devices through artificial intelligence (AI)-based object detection. A custom-trained model was used to recognize a predefined set of objects, and the detected items are displayed in the AR environment together with descriptive information retrieved from a database. On the other hand, the same application supports covert communication by allowing users to hide and retrieve secret files within an augmented reality setting. To achieve these goals, we first examined augmented reality, including its background, commonly used techniques, current applications and expected future developments. We then reviewed key information security methods, with particular attention to steganography and cryptography. Based on this foundation, the AES algorithm was applied for data encryption, while the LSB technique was used to hide information within images. These elements were combined into an AI-powered AR image steganography application. Although the system appears to function as a standard object detection and AR application, it also includes hidden communication capabilities.

Several directions for future work have been identified. Further training and adjustment of the AI model are planned to improve detection accuracy. In addition, the process of extracting hidden data will be refined to make it more efficient and reliable. Furthermore, deploying the application on a server and introducing a subscription-based service would allow users to share QR codes that point to specific logical spaces where authorized recipients can access hidden information. To enhance security, future versions of the system will explore the use of generative adversarial networks for image steganography, replacing the traditional LSB method. Finally, integrating generative AI APIs would enable the automatic generation of more detailed descriptions of detected objects.

DOI: 10.1201/9781042003860-8

Index

For Product Safety Concerns and Information please contact our EU representative GPSR@taylorandfrancis.com Taylor & Francis Verlag GmbH, Kaufingerstraße 24, 80331 München, Germany